THE PERENNIAL GARDEN

THE PERENNIAL GARDEN

MICHAEL KING

MITCHELL BEAZLEY

THE PERENNIAL GARDEN
Michael King

First published in Great Britain in 2006
by Mitchell Beazley, an imprint of
Octopus Publishing Group Limited
2–4 Heron Quays, London E14 4JP

A CIP catalogue copy of this book is available
from the British Library

ISBN 1 84533 175 3

Commissioning Editor: Michèle Byam
Art Editor: Victoria Burley
Design: Kate Ward
Photography: Michael King
Production: Jane Rogers
Index: Sue Farr

Printed and bound in China by
Toppan Printing Company Limited

HALF TITLE *Astrantia major*
'Claret'

TITLE PAGE *Eryngium* x
tripartitum

CONTENTS PAGE A park
border in Stockholm,
designed by Ulf Nordfjell.

Contents

Preface

Hardy herbaceous perennials are the transient, ephemeral elements that introduce not only colour, textures, and form to gardens but also bring a dynamic vitality to their design when each year they appear, perform, and disappear again within the more stable framework of walls, hedges, paths, and lawns. For many gardeners perennials are simply a means of adding colour; once they finish flowering they hold no more interest until next year's repeat performance. For me these plants hold far more potential. Their precocious shoots in spring are eagerly awaited and signal the start of a complex process of growth and interaction. Their flowering may be spectacular, but this can only last for so long; if the plant is going to earn its place in a garden it must contribute more. Character is the word I use to embrace the effect a plant may have on its surroundings and the people who encounter it. The art of planting design is in recognizing this and using the plant in the garden in positions and associations that emphasize and exploit its character to the full.

This book shows how perennials can enhance your garden by drawing you in their direction and communicating your passions and aspirations. It does not, however, seek to be a catalogue of perennials – there are many splendid books of these already. The first part of *The Perennial Garden* is concerned with garden design in general and the role that perennials can play within this. In certain situations perennials alone can make a garden, but this is rarely the case. Normally they are used within a garden framework, so there are examples to demonstrate how they can be related to such settings.

The second half of the book provides some thematic plantings. Here individual plants reign supreme and are grouped by season or the situations in which they are most effective. Drawing on visits to many different gardens, some professionally designed, others created by talented gardeners, the text and illustrations combine to show what worked well and what inspired me. Gardening, like life, has its constraints and from the range of possibilities revealed in these pages I hope to identify ideas that appeal and inspire gardeners to do something different and original in their own gardens.

Michael King, Amsterdam, 2006

Designing with Perennials

Some Principles of Garden Design

The country residence of American landscape architect James van Sweden overlooks the waters of Chesapeake Bay in Maryland. The adjacent wetland meadow fuses with the naturalistic garden planting of native grasses and perennials, which is brought right up to the edge of the decking (*left*). Here in mid-summer, drifts of the blue grass (*Schizachyrium scoparium*) contrasts with green clumps of *Panicum virgatum*. Yellow-flowered *Silphium perfoliatum* luxuriates in the heat and humidity found here in mid-summer. Clearly at home, it has self-seeded throughout the garden and dominates, so will need controlling to retain the planting scheme's integrity.

PREVIOUS PAGES Within the old walls of the vegetable garden at Scampston Hall in North Yorkshire, England, the Dutch designer Piet Oudolf has created a contemporary garden seen here in mellow morning light in mid-summer. The view is dominated by the light green grass *Sesleria autumnalis* and clumps of purple *Monarda* 'Aquarius'.

The desire to create a garden is bound up with the need for refuge, and its origins go back further than history can record. The form that a garden takes has varied from land to land – as have the plants it contained – and over time many influences have been brought to bear on its appearance. Real gardens do not exist in a vacuum but are situated in a specific landscape and will often complement any adjacent buildings – and the plants they contain must be able to cope with the local climate and other environmental conditions. In every case their final appearance will have been influenced by their location.

CULTURE AND CLIMATE

In the broadest sense, a garden is located within a specific cultural context. The national identity of a country, together with the attitudes and aspirations of its people, should have an impact on the final design of any new garden located there. In Australia, for example, water shortages, the increased prevalence of bush fires, and a growing awareness of environmental issues have boosted the popularity of native-plant gardens in recent years. At their best, these use endemic plants in organized patterns to integrate housing with the local landscape. They aim to produce a result that is

aesthetically pleasing, in harmony with its surroundings, and satisfying to its owners who wish to establish a link with their floral heritage. Conversely, the Japanese garden in Europe is an example of what can go wrong when a design ignores its location's cultural context. Whereas they are splendid exhibits of a particular gardening style in Japan, they all too often look out of place when isolated from their true origins.

Garden-making in western Europe offers its own opportunities. In Britain, reference is often made to "the continental style of planting". Yet on the European mainland there are many difference between the French, Dutch, and German garden styles, and these are essential if their gardens are to exist in harmony with all aspects of their surroundings. Even within a single country, there are regional variations which are partly due to diversities in topography and climate and partly to local differences between the indigenous peoples and their lifestyles.

As with culture, a garden designer cannot ignore the prevailing climatic conditions, which vary from country to country and place to place, especially as people attempt to garden in locations as different as the seeringly hot Arizona desert and the frozen wastes of Iceland. Whenever the plants themselves form the heart of a design, a

The landscape architect Kathryn Gustafson, the artist Robert Israel, and the plantsman Piet Oudolf have designed the Lurie Garden as part of the Millennium Park project on the lakeside in downtown Chicago. It is located on the roof of a huge car park, and its setting is overtly urban. The planting, however, makes reference to the once-extensive prairies that grew here in Midwest America. The Indian (*Panicum*) and little blue stem (*Schizachyrium*) grasses are two native species featured prominently.

White (*top left*) and purple coneflowers (*Echinacea*) bring colour, while *Eryngium yuccifolium* (*right*) adds spiky seed heads for contrast and accent. But not everything here is native as this is a park, not a nature reserve. For example, the pink pompoms of the common European onion *Allium senescens* subsp. *montanum* 'Summer Beauty' (*bottom left*), rusty toned Oriental daylilies (*Hemerocallis*) (*above*), and other perennial cultivars and exotics help to create a long season of visual delights for visitors.

ABOVE Joe Pye weed (*Eupatorium purpureum* subsp. *maculatum* 'Gateway'), a native in the Mississippi valley, looks good when mass-planted beside the decking, while ornamental grasses help the garden merge into the wild meadow beyond.

LEFT Perennials and in particular here evergreen *Liriope muscari* emphasize this garden's layout.

multitude of factors will influence what can be grown there: the weather, the soil conditions, exposure to wind, and seasonal temperatures. Attempts to oppose these factors can be successful but all too often create a sense of artificiality. The most effective planting designs use plants suited to the existing conditions; these may be native to the country in question or exotics from other locations in the world that share the same environmental conditions.

CONTEXT AND ART
Another aspect of a garden's location more often than not dominates its design. This is

that the garden's design has to fit the context of the buildings it surrounds. Gardens are usually associated with houses or other buildings and can be used either to extend living space into the outdoors or to provide a setting for the architecture. Paths run from the boundary to the main entrance, focal points and features need to be visible from the windows, and sitting areas should be next to convenient access points.

The world outside the garden's boundaries may also play a role. In the city, the surrounding landscape will normally be buildings in differing styles and scales. In the countryside, the setting may be open and less formal. Either way, the garden's design must either incorporate such influences or assertively exclude them.

Although a garden's location plays a key role in determining its design, it does place a raft of restrictions and limitations on the gardener's aspirations. After taking all of this on board, the creative process must overcome such constraints, just as the painter must overcome the limitations of a flat canvas and its frame or the potter must devise ways to manipulate his clay.

The garden designer may already appear to be overwhelmed by constraints. Yet there is yet another factor that must be added to the equation, namely the people who will actually be using the garden. The garden may be just for you yourself, for a family or small group of people, or for the general public, as in the case of a park. And in every case the user will bring to the design brief his or her own aspirations. Personal tastes, prejudices, and associations are all capable of generating very powerful emotions and must somehow be accommodated, as well as any practical requirements. Such constraints should not inhibit the creative process but rather be used to stimulate it. Yet can the end result ever aspire to being a work of art if its basis is so grounded in practical matters of location and personal approval?

Fortunately, the garden maker's constraints are no more limiting than those experienced by the painter or potter. In addition, garden designers have one medium for expression that is unique to them: living plant material – and perennials in particular. Outdoor spaces can of course be made without plants, a good example of which would be a city square, but these fall outside most definitions of a garden. A true garden has a will and energy of its own. Unlike paint or clay, the plants it contains are alive, and gardeners seem able to form an emotional bond with them, irrational as this may seem.

Responses to individual plants vary. The most immediate reactions occur through the

associations attached to certain plants. Sunflowers may remind you of summer and your childhood, for example, and roses of a special person. Thrift may recall clifftop walks on a holiday. Following these initial reactions, you may decide to seek out relationships which reinforce your memories. Do the sunflowers peep over the garden wall as you remember them? Do the roses grow in the same sort of formal patterns that reflect

your memories? Does the thrift hang down from craggy outcrops or is it merely lying flat on the ground? Many of these associations are nostalgic, but others will be evocative. Palm trees and bamboo immediately signal exotic places, while foxgloves and pinks suggest an idealized cottage garden. In every case, however, you are reacting to the plant as an individual and not merely as an inanimate object.

Beyond such immediate responses, the plants in a garden may engage you in many other ways. Buds burst open and shoots appear in spring. Foliage emerges fresh, matures, and maybe flushes with autumn tints before falling to the ground. Flowers blossom and then die. Although it is imperceptible, you are subconsciously aware that whatever you look at is changing. You know that what you see today will have

Agastache foeniculum is a common garden plant in Europe, yet in the Lurie Garden in Chicago it has been included because it is a wildflower of the region.

ABOVE A simple pavilion creates the threshold to this garden while serving as part of the enclosure once its steps have been negotiated. Bold clumps of *Salvia nemorosa* 'Ostfriesland' have been placed in front to draw attention to the entrance and encourage visitors to enter into it.

LEFT Drifts of coneflowers (*Echinacea*) and shrubby *Perovskia atriplicifolia* 'Blue Spire', together with ornamental grasses, bring a wash of colour to the lakeside at the Chicago Botanic Garden. Such bold drifts of perennials are the hallmarks of the designers Wolfgang Oehme and James van Sweden.

changed by tomorrow and may be gone completely just a week later. This transience of garden effects implores you to stop, look, and savour the scene. Such moments are intimate as you consciously develop a bond with the plants in a way that could never occur with paint or clay. Over time you find yourself celebrating your plant's successes and mourning their failures; they become an integral part of your lives.

As living organisms, plants are at the mercy of natural forces such as wind, rain, and snow. At times you fear for their lives and often marvel at their resilience. In autumn your heart may jump when you see tall grasses flapping like flags with the wind ripping through their foliage and their flower heads glinting in the low-angled sunlight. With their help, you can feel in touch with reality.

Individually, and as a chorus, plants seem capable of engaging our senses and emotions, and a garden creates a forum in which this can occur. The interaction is in effect at a one-to-one level and calls for intimacy and seclusion. Time and tranquillity are needed to look and appreciate the scene before you in a way that would never occur if you stood in the same spot as part of a group. For this reason, when designing gardens, I have developed the concept of the threshold. Sometimes this can take the form of a gate, an arch, or pathway, although a change in level or planting style is sufficient. Whether it exists physically or not, for me the real garden begins where functional spaces end and where there is room to stop and think.

Planting Design

Flower spikes of *Digitalis ferruginea* and the drumsticks of *Allium sphaerocephalon* add interest without disturbing the bold drift of *Deschampsia cespitosa* 'Goldtau', which creates an open space in this English country garden.

Perennials are only a part of the garden maker's toolbox, because, when designing, their relationship to everything around them is of paramount concern. Beyond the wider concerns of culture, climate, context, and art, the perennials you choose for your garden will be there for practical reasons, such as groundcover, screens, or colourful spectacle, or because they are being grown for a host of artistic and emotional motives to control the mood of the spaces they occupy and delight your senses with their pleasing forms, colours, scents, or associations. Before delving into the details of plant form, texture, and colour, which more usually underpin any discussion of planting design, you need to stand back and look at the larger picture to see how perennials can work alongside the other elements that might be used to create a garden space.

Structure

As a whole, a garden needs an underlying structure that relates it to its location and any buildings it may contain. Walls, paths, lawns, and open water together with trees, shrubs, and hedges combine to create a three-dimensional space. Tall-growing perennials might be massed to function in the same way, even though they may not be effective throughout the whole year. Alternatively, low-growing perennials may be used to highlight the ground plan or to introduce focal points that draw you into its recesses.

As part of the building blocks of a garden's design, perennials can play a significant role in the interplay between masses and voids, which is crucial to the organization and feel of any outdoor space. The stiff upright grass *Calamagrostis* x *acutiflora* is perfect for this when it is planted in large blocks or lines. In early spring low mounds of foliage create effective groundcover, but in early summer it

The front garden at Bury Court in England has been designed by Christopher Bradley-Hole. Reminiscent of the logical arrangement of a botanic garden, flowerbeds of various sizes interact with the buildings that surround the space. Here in early summer golden-flowered *Stipa gigantea* creates a setting for flowering lilies and red hot pokers (*Kniphofia*). Water reflects the open sky and prevents the area from feeling cluttered (*right*). Elsewhere in the garden (*above*), solid blocks of *Calamagrostis* x *acutiflora* 'Karl Foerster' line the path leading to the front door.

shoots into flower, blocking out the view, and dynamically altering the architecture of the space it occupies. Alternatively, tall-growing purple moor grasses (*Molinia caerulea* subsp. *arundinacea*) can throw up see-through screens of flower stems in mid-summer, to create less obtrusive barriers (*see p.169*). The paddle-shaped leaves of bergenias and the strap-like blades of woodrushes are examples of evergreen perennials that can effectively outline a garden's routes or be assembled to fill out its voids.

The planting itself needs an underlying structure, in exactly the same way as the whole garden. Without it, the plants create an amorphous mass. Contrasts introduce interplay between the components, with dominant elements counterbalanced by neutral zones, which function as the voids on a more intimate scale.

Plant Characteristics

The size and shapes of perennials are as varied as any other group of plants. Eupatoriums, macleayas, and many grasses and bamboos can tower well above your head, while thymes, sedums, and a host of popular perennials remain below knee and even ankle height. The flower heads of many perennials are their most significant features, and when these are slim and upright they attract attention, functioning as visual full stops.

It is too easy to become absorbed by the detailed beauty of a plant without objectively considering its garden impact. Proportion and scale are therefore fundamental to planting design. Some plants need to be planted in generous groups to hold their own against more dominant neighbours. This scaling-up can quickly cause pressure on available space, but your aim should be to create an effective garden picture and not to provide a collection of disparate plants. Inevitably, fewer different types of plants can be used in any given area, but if their relationships to one another are carefully orchestrated the result will have greater impact.

The size of plants used in any given space also needs consideration. Large plants and plants with bold foliage should not be excluded from small spaces. Their effect is often the opposite of expectations. The simplification in the planting palette that they automatically impose creates a greater feeling of space – their wider unfussy leaves introducing a relaxed mood into intimate spaces. Conversely, smaller, finely textured plants planted en masse in larger areas can intensify the feeling of openness.

RIGHT Perennials do not come much bigger than *Persicaria polymorpha*. Here it has been repeated with dramatic effect in the Square Garden at Waltham Place, England, by the Dutch garden designer Henk Gerritsen. *Salvia* x *superba* 'Dear Anja' adds a splash of colour this early in summer.

LEFT A large block of *Calamagrostis* x *acutiflora* 'Overdam' prevents this small garden from becoming cluttered. Red-flowered *Astilbe* 'Fanal' skirts its ankles, while silver-leaved *Artemisia ludoviciana* subsp. *ludoviciana* var. *latiloba* and yellow *Anthemis tinctoria* 'Lemon Maid' are the focus of attention.

Combining Shapes, Textures, and Colour

Perennial plants can have a rounded or upright growth habit. Their flowers may be held in a rounded cluster or in erect flower heads. Leaves on perennials may be heavy and dense, or develop in a fine, light, and see-through manner. Other perennials produce smooth, furry, spiky, and rough-textured leaves – all interesting characteristics to exploit in planting associations.

However, more than any one of the aforementioned perennial attributes, their considerable variation in leaf, flower, or stem colours is prized most highly by gardeners. These different qualities form the basis for developing associations when creating successful planting schemes.

LEFT The upright habit of *Iris sibirica* 'Perry's Blue' contrasts with the colour and mounded form of *Euphorbia palustris*, the dark leaves of *Ligularia dentata* 'Desdemona', and the textured fern fronds.

BELOW The round spiky flower heads of echinops are yet another distinctive shape with which to accent planting schemes.

TOP LEFT Waist-high, rounded clumps of flower and foliage are effectively supplied by *Miscanthus sinensis* 'Yaku-jima'.

CENTRE LEFT Harmonized through their shared colouring, this euphorbia, hosta, and grass (*Melica uniflora* f. *albida*) create an intriguing combination of contrasting textures.

BOTTOM LEFT When planted together, *Rodgersia podophylla* and frothy *Ranunculus aconitifolius* 'Flore Pleno' provide an eye-catching contrast of colours and form.

ABOVE The slim flower spikes of *Verbena hastata* stand out against the frothy blossom of x *Solidaster luteus* 'Lemore'.

A single plant will be eye-catching when its shape is distinctive. A neat, rounded clump of *Euphorbia polychroma* holds the eye, and when placed on the corner of a border or at the junction of two paths it will tend to stop your visual progress. Two such distinctive forms when planted side by side will focus your attention on the central point between the pair, to a path or entrance, for example. When three or any odd number of these same plants are positioned together, the human brain is unable to pair them off and so registers them as a group.

The same is true with distinctive upright plants such as verbascums and eremurus. A single plant leads the eye upwards, a pair focuses attention on what lies between them, and three or more upright plants form a clump of verticals with potential for adding contrasting combinations with horizontal forms.

This balanced, or neutral, association of forms comprises tall, rounded *Eupatorium purpureum* subsp. *maculatum* 'Gateway', the lower, rounded grass *Pennisetum alopecuroides*, and vertical *Calamagrostis* x *acutiflora* 'Karl Foerster'.

When the shapes or textures of adjacent plants are similar they are said to harmonize. Harmonious perennials create a peaceful atmosphere, and the same is true with similarly coloured ones. The opposite is naturally true, so that when for example something spiky is grown next to a soft rounded plant the contrast in form or texture is highlighted. Spiky forms alone seem more stimulating and noticeable than lower, rounded shapes, and it is these types of relationships that are at the core of all planting design. However, while the design concepts are really relatively simple, with only so many perennials available, the choice of which to use is not.

Plant selection will be determined by other factors relating to the situation and the planting theme you are developing. When deciding on the quantities of individual plants for any planting scheme, you should also consider the effect you want to achieve.

All too often planting combinations are developed with an even mix of contrasting and harmonizing shapes. Two rounded forms of differing heights and one upright is almost a cliché: for example a tall and billowing *Campanula lactiflora*, a low and round *Alchemilla mollis*, and a spiky, upright flowering delphinium. Such a group might be described as balanced, which in fact it is, but the visual effect is as a consequence neutral.

However, if a planting scheme is to communicate an idea or evoke an emotional response in terms of mood and atmosphere, you need to adapt the way its components are orchestrated. By using the same plants in various proportions, different visual effects become possible.

Imagine massive islands of the already mentioned, soft blue campanula surrounded by a swirling sea of foaming alchemilla with here and there dark jets of delphiniums erupting out of it, and already you are starting on a journey of gardening adventure and discovery. Arrange the cast differently and the storyline instantly alters. Billowing clouds of misty blue campanulas can serve as a background to dozens of spiky delphiniums rising out of a wide plain of alchemilla, to create a scene as vigorous and dramatic as the Manhattan skyline.

Analogies with the composition of music can be drawn in the ways that you might arrange harmonies and contrasts, or areas of peace or high drama throughout a garden. As with music, crescendos need to follow on from stiller passages in which themes recur and are reinterpreted. An even mix of the two would be dull, and an overemphasis on either might become tedious. If possible, your garden should follow a score with each feature following on from the next in a sequence that ebbs and flows between ideas and moods and thereby rewards those who pass through with new and varied ideas.

Design combinations should not only be thought of in the horizontal plane, with plants set out in clumps or drifts side by side, but also in the vertical. In nature plant communities are composed of plants of differing statures. The clearest example of this is mature woodland, where the trees create the top tier; beneath these grow shrubs, saplings, and maybe shorter tree species. Lower still flourish the shade-tolerant perennials, which in turn may occupy the same soil as lower-growing, spring-flowering bulbs, and perennials that complete their growth cycles early in the year before being overshadowed by their companions.

In the garden your planting scheme will gain greater complexity and interest when you follow the same layered approach. Schemes may use the same mix of woody and herbaceous material, but even within the herbaceous layer such relationships can be developed. Plumes of aruncus blossom might float above mounds of *Geranium pratense*. At a lower level, ferns or soloman's seal (*Polygonatum*) might arch out over carpets of fine-textured groundcover such as *Leptinella*

The romance of the meadow has been created using misty *Deschampsia cespitosa* 'Goldschleier' and scabious such as *Knautia macedonica*.

squalida 'Platt's Black' or *Lysimachia nummularia* 'Aurea'.

Plants originating from similar habitats commonly share characteristics and so lead to harmonious combinations when they are used together in the garden. Through association, your mind will often reinforce such harmonies and expand the range of potential partners to include all other elements your experiences would associate with such places. Plants from the meadow such as scabious, astrantia, thalictrum, and coreopsis will as a consequence look natural when growing in association with ornamental grasses, even when their true homelands may be continents apart. Likewise, bamboo, gunnera, and tree ferns find unity in the mind's eye of the gardener passionate about the abundant variety more generally associated with the rainforest.

Rhythm and Repetition

Rhythms are present at all levels in the outside garden: when you walk, pause, breath, and stare; when plants grow, flower, and die; in the weather cycles; and when time moves inexorably forwards. Some rhythms are general and all-embracing, such as the changing seasons, while others are intimate and revealed only through study and contemplation. There is also rhythm in the shape and forms of plants: the arrangement of leaves on stems, of petals in flowers, and in seed heads. All of this may guide your hand when arranging plants in your garden.

The interplay of harmonies and contrasts needs organizing in the planting plan, as it does on the page of a musical score. Rhythm is created by repetition. In formal designs

ABOVE The mirror borders at Bramdean House are in perfect symmetry. In early summer blue delphiniums and clumps of catmint are planted at regular intervals.

LEFT Cohesion through repetition gives this informal planting dramatic impact. Its highlights are purple monardas, rusty red heleniums, and yellow *Rudbeckia maxima*.

FOLLOWING PAGES A straight, stepped path with trees arranged at regular intervals is both softened and unified by the irregular repetition of similar rounded forms and also the same plants set along its length. These include the evergreen *Euphorbia characias* subsp. *wulfenii* and the contrasting spikes of violet-purple *Salvia pratensis* 'Indigo'.

TOP The flowering of *Nepeta* 'Six Hills Giant' signals the start of summer in the garden.

ABOVE Bedding perennials have here been used to provide a modern twist to the tradition of formal parks in late summer. *Miscanthus sinensis* 'Kleine Fontäne' lines up along the back, while upright, shrubby *Perovskia atriplicifolia* 'Blue Spire' fills the foreground. In between, there is a raging torrent of foaming x *Solidaster* 'Super' punctuated by dark-toned *Echinacea purpurea*.

plants will be repeated at regular intervals and in even numbers. Such a style brings harmony through logic, balance, and the reassurance of its simple beat. When rhythms vary their pace and pattern, they can transform the atmosphere of a garden from slow, regular, and peaceful to one that is fast, variable, and exciting. "Planting in which rhythmic potential is realized is planting that will stir the spirit", as Lucy Gent eloquently stated in her classic book *Great Planting*.

Progress within a garden – be this the route you follow on foot or the zigzag line along which the eye moves as it interprets what lies before it – will be controlled by the repetitions within its design. The same plant might be repeated throughout the garden as a signpost. Alternatively, similarity of form or colour can be sufficient to achieve the same result. The upright flower stems of delphiniums may be mirrored by the dark purple shafts of *Liatris spicata* and elsewhere the flower spikes of *Dictamnus albus*. Not only is this a more interesting way to design a garden but it also enables you to maintain a planting rhythm when different growing conditions occur in various parts of the garden.

Through repetition, planting themes become reinforced and gain impact. However, the more one plant is used, the more other possibilities are excluded. In order to retain a theme and rhythm, planting schemes need to be simple yet clearly focused.

Large clumps of red hot pokers (*Kniphofia*) and red *Monarda* 'Squaw' unite a long, thin border into a single coherent unit within this garden's design.

Arranging Border Planting Schemes

When perennials are grown in front of a wall or hedge it is logical to place the taller-growing plants at the back and progressively shorter ones towards the front. However such a design can look boring, so garden design books may suggest having an occasional break in this arrangement. While this is something that most gardeners work out for themselves, another almost more important design point is often overlooked, namely how the plants that perform at different times of the year should be placed within the border.

Some perennials die down shortly after flowering, leaving gaps in a planting area that must be filled in some way. Examples of these include aquilegia, corydalis, *Crambe cordifolia*, *Dicentra spectabilis*, doronicum, *Papaver orientale*, *Primula sieboldii*, and *Thalictrum aquilegiifolium*. Clearly if such plants are planted in large groups they will eventually create large gaps in the border. One way of concealing these is to plant other perennials nearby that start into growth relatively late, such as hostas, which might

This carefully arranged border places every plant to best advantage, in a cascade. Deschampsia grass flowers in the foreground, and the flat flower heads of *Achillea* 'Walther Funcke' contrast with the violet-purple flower spikes of *Salvia x sylvestris* 'Tänzerin' and the taller-growing *Veronicastrum virginicum* 'Lavendelturm'. The flower heads of *Monarda* 'Gardenview Scarlet' have sharp outlines, while the opposite is true of the frothy, pale yellow flowers of *Thalictrum lucidum* next to it. This border will look just as interesting in winter, when the plants have formed seed heads and become dormant.

However, too many of these late perennials growing together escalates the gappy problem and so is best avoided.

There is a temptation to plant early flowering perennials towards the front of a border, where these lower-growing plants can brighten up the foreground and receive full attention. Once their main season of interest is over, however, they make little contribution for the rest of the growing season so their prime position is rather wasted. The low stature of early flowering perennials and bulbs is better farther back in a border, because at this time of the year there is little else growing tall enough to obstruct the view.

Early flowering perennials such as pulmonarias, brunneras, dicentras, and aquilegias are truly plants of the woodland edge and look their best growing in and around the base of trees and shrubs, especially when these woody plants form the background to a border. Also many spring-flowering bulbs such as winter aconites, snowdrops, scillas, and grape hyacinths fall into this category. All are best used in drifts at the back of borders and filling gaps between and under shrubs, where they take advantage of the relatively high light levels prior to the arrival of shade from the developing leaf canopy.

Conversely, as the growing season progresses the plants in the border grow taller and fill out the available space, so if any late flowering plant is to be seen properly it should positioned well forward within the planting scheme. For example, asters are indispensable for their late-season colour, and when these are relatively low growing they need to be placed at the very front of a border. Their dull appearance through spring and summer can easily be overcome by mixing them with other plants that draw attention away from them at such times, including bulbs such as tulips in spring and alliums in summer.

Beyond the pragmatism of placing plants in borders where they will be seen, the

rise up and cover for example the fading foliage of *Corydalis cava* in a woodland scheme. In an open sunny border *Gypsophila paniculata* might be positioned so that it throws up its billowing cloud of flowering stems in time to replace the holes left by bulky clumps of oriental poppy foliage.

Gaps in borders earlier in the season which are created by perennials that are slow to come into growth and make an impact, such as *Eupatorium purpureum* and warm-season grasses such as *Miscanthus sinensis*, are usually less of a problem as spring-flowering bulbs can be grown nearby.

patterns and repetitions in which they are arranged will have a huge impact on the overall appearance of the planting scheme. The traditional English herbaceous border presents the plants in clearly arranged groups that may harmonize or alternatively contrast with one another by way of their flower colours, shapes, and/or heights and textures. The size and shapes of these groups may vary depending on the types of perennials grown, the size of the borders, and the artistic intentions of the gardener. The double mirror borders at Bramdean House, Hampshire, England (*see p.33*), for example, rely for their success not only on the diligent control of the size and relationships of the perennials growing adjacent to one another but also on their repetition on either side of the grass path.

Large blocks of perennials have their drawbacks. They create gaps that can disturb the border's impact when, for example, flowers are their main justification for inclusion or when they require a rigorous prune in the middle of the growing season to rejuvenate their foliage – as is the best way of managing sprawling hardy geraniums and *Alchemilla mollis*. To avoid this it is a good idea to stretch the groups out into what is often called drifts. This weaving together of a border's components creates a softer effect so when any one area loses impact it is effectively disguised by its neighbours.

One step further in mixing perennials in borders is to arrange them in repeating groups, or singly even, as might be encountered in a natural plant community such as a meadow. I have experimented with borders that I conceive as discrete units within a garden's design. The plants they contain are mixed evenly to create a uniform impression rather than the changes and variations that occur across conventional flower borders. These borders are an attempt to find a contemporary solution for domestic-

ABOVE Perennials have been arranged in this border in both blocks and drifts in the traditional manner. Starting from the front, they are *Echinacea purpurea* 'Magnus', blue *Perovskia atriplicifolia* 'Blue Spire', *Aster amellus* 'King George', *Monarda* 'Blaustrumpf', and *Agastache* 'Blue Fortune'.

BELOW In this 600m (2,000ft) long border Heiner Luz has used a mixture of perennials to create a long season of interest. The dominant species flower in sequence from spring to autumn. They are *Primula veris, Iris sibirica, Nepeta sibirica, Veronica longifolia, Mentha suaveolens*, and *Boltonia asteroides* var. *latisquama* with *Aster laevis*. These species are supplemented by others to increase diversity and interest, among which are mint (*Mentha*), *Alchemilla epipsila, Geranium wlassovianum, Camassia cusickii, Lythrum salicaria, Sanguisorba officinalis, Molinia caerulea* subsp. *arundinacea*, and quite noticeable in this image the umbrella flower heads of *Valeriana officinalis*.

scale gardens, where the flower borders form part of a simple architectural plan but have greater complexity and seasonal interest than might be found in the minimalist planting schemes in public spaces where, for example, a single species may be used in wide drifts. One freestanding border, for example, contained every cultivar and species of echinacea that I could find. This was its theme. Grasses such as *Panicum virgatum* and *Sporobolus heterolepis* were added not only to create a visual contrast with the bold, cone-centred flowers of the echinaceas but also to signal the prairie homeland of these flowers, which were the underlying inspiration for the border. The other plants included, such as *Salvia nemorosa, S. verticillata*, and the low, silver-leaved clumps of *Anaphalis triplinervis*, were there to provide early summer interest and structure. For spring interest, these perennials were generously interplanted with pure red tulips.

A similar approach has been perfected by the German landscape architect Heiner Luz for application in huge-scale public projects in which he has specialized; he terms it the leading-aspect system. Heiner Luz considers the conventional herbaceous border an inappropriate concept for contemporary public spaces but recognizes the potential of perennials to engage and delight people. The mixtures he creates are planted out to form discrete, uniform blocks of vegetation within the urban landscape.

Having established the circumstances of the available growing conditions, in particular soil type and moisture levels, Heiner Luz designs mixtures of appropriate perennials; these fall into one of two groups. The first and most numerous group, comprising up to 75 percent of the total, are the leading-aspect perennials. These, creating the dominant image of the planting, are chosen to produce a sequence of flower or foliage

ABOVE **ABOVE** In this second example of his work, Heiner Luz uses plants adapted to a wet yet very free-draining site. At this time in high summer colour is subdued, yet the interplay of greens is stunning. The bushy clumps of *Aster sedifolius* dominate, even though they have yet to come into flower. In autumn, they will turn this slope into a sheet of lavender-blue. In total there are seven species making up the leading-aspect perennials in this scheme and some ten more secondary species.

LEFT This simpler Heiner Luz scheme introduces grasses with a long seasonal impact. Here in mid-summer *Stipa calamagrostis* 'Lemperg' dominates together with blue *Nepeta sibirica*. Prairie dropseed grass (*Sporobolus heterolepis*) flowers later and will turn a glorious shade of ochre in autumn, when the chrysanthemum *Leucanthemella serotina* sprinkles its single white flowers across the horizon.

interest throughout the growing season. The secondary group complement the leading-aspect perennials in season by adding variety. They are generally most effective when viewed from nearby. For this reason the distribution of the secondary group of perennials may well vary throughout the planting area to distinguish its different parts and locations.

There will be five to eight species making up each of these two groups, with some plants being repeated more than once per square metre, while others appear only every 6–8sq m (65–85sq ft). Heiner Luz's system has been developed to allow very efficient planting, with the plants being arranged on the ground first according to their numbers per square metre. Approximately, twelve plants per square metre are used.

In order to minimize maintenance, the ground is heavily mulched with gravel after planting. In the early stages more interventions are needed to remove weeds and water in dry periods. After some three years the plants form a closed blanket, and maintenance is little more than the removal of the dead top-growth early each spring and a general tidying up.

The art to making these mixtures lies not only in finding plants that grow well and flower in sequence but also in taking into account their individual characteristics to ensure that outside their main season they still contribute positively to the overall effect. Seed heads, autumn tints, and silhouettes all need to be assessed to create a scheme that is effective through the whole year.

Planting in Time and Space

The sequence in which changes occur within a garden are one of its underlying rhythms. In the largest gardens this can mean certain areas are set aside for climaxes at different times of the year: the vernal or spring garden, the summer rose parterre, and the late-summer dahlia border may be familiar themes. In smaller gardens, space is at a premium and no area can be ignored for a major part of the year. Conversely, any attempt to make the entire garden interesting all year will fail as the display will become diluted across the garden canvas because it lacks any rhythm or focus. My solution has been to design different parts of my own garden so they become the focus of attention at separate times of year.

The garden by the entrance gate is interesting from the moment the snowdrops come into flower in winter right through to spring, with the arrival of other bulbs and companion perennials and shrubs. In summer it would assume a less dominant role, providing a quite green oasis, as by then other parts of the garden are calling out for attention. Steadily the centre of focus moves around, yet a sense of unity is maintained by the repetition of certain key elements

RIGHT This border in my own garden in early summer has a long season of interest. At this time it reaches a subtle climax with the flowering of *Persicaria polymorpha* (at the back) and *Aruncus dioicus* 'Zweiweltenkind' (centre). The bright colour of *Geranium* 'Patricia' adds sparkle, and by using this same plant in other parts of the garden I am able to establish a link between all of its areas. Later, eupatoriums, heleniums, asters, and miscanthus grasses come into flower and so provide a change of mood.

BELOW Huge perennials such as *Eupatorium purpureum* subsp. *maculatum* 'Atropurpureum' tower above the head and add grandeur to a late summer border in this garden.

throughout the whole garden both within and beyond the main point of climax.

For many people, the main pleasure of a garden comes from experiencing the changing seasons. Perennials that typically die down in winter are some of the most dynamic elements in any garden. I love large and tall perennials such as eupatoriums, persicarias, and helianthus, which can so dramatically alter the volumes

within a border in the course of just one growing season. The big tidy-up in spring is an equal pleasure when growing such monsters and is all part of the forceful nature of perennial plant gardening, from the freedom of the open field to enclosure and overwhelming grandeur and back to openness again. For me, this cycle is more enticing than any perfect day in summer when everything is flowering as hoped for.

On of the great challenges of garden art is this changeable nature of the plants which are at its heart. Living plant material is never entirely predictable, and its behaviour is affected by many factors outside the influence of the garden maker, such as weather, infestation, and disease. Coping with this lack of control is part of the art. It introduces spontaneity and risk. But beyond these seasonal variations, one factor that is

unique to the art of gardening is the process of maturation. Plants grow, age, and die. Trees grow taller, casting ever more shade on their surroundings and affecting what can be grown nearby. Perennials may spread and begin to compete with their neighbours. Day by day and year on year, gardens inexorably experience change, and you as a gardener need to understand this and plan accordingly.

When gardening is seen as a process in which you engage with nature, rather than an activity to make something perfect and permanent, any drawbacks that time and maturation may introduce instantly vanish. I have planted many trees in my own garden. Deliberately I used small saplings. Five years ago they cast almost no shade. The borders they are associated with contained sun-loving perennials such as veronicas, phlox, salvias, and anthemis. Year on year the shade increased, so one by one the perennials in these borders had to be changed. Hardy

geraniums are continuing to thrive, but the verticals of veronicas have been replaced with *Actaea simplex* and *Astilbe chinensis* var. *taquetii* 'Purpurlanze'. Over time this area of my garden will become simpler as shade increases, and what were borders filled with summer colour will evolve into a tranquil shady retreat.

One step beyond maturation is death and after this is decay. This is the reality of true nature and may not always be welcomed. Planting design is as much about exclusion as it is about selection, and for each of us the limits will differ. Nobody tidies up nature in spring as gardeners feel obliged to do in their gardens. But choices must be made because gardening, like art, is an expression of an idea and not a true representation of nature.

The traditional herbaceous border is at one end of a spectrum where plants from a range of different habitats are grown together in highly controlled conditions for purely

ABOVE A domesticated form of rosebay willowherb or fireweed (*Chamerion angustifolium* 'Album', syn *Epilobium angustifolium* 'Album') blurs the boundary of this countryside garden. This garden perennial is a less aggressive spreader than its parent, but that is only relatively speaking. In a border it will need managing unless wild abandon is your aim.

BELOW The steppe-type habitat is characterized by poor, gravelly, well-drained soil in baking sunshine. This slope at Lady Farm, England offers similar conditions and has been planted in a contemporary naturalistic style, using drought-tolerant grasses and perennial achilleas, red hot pokers, and biennial verbascums. Maintenance is minimal, yet the display of flower colour, seed heads, and silhouettes brings year-round interest.

aesthetic reasons. Plant growth is tamed and tied, and every few years the plants are divided and replanted to maintain their relationships with one another – in other words, to halt the process of maturation.

Alternative approaches have emerged in recent years involving less intervention. By avoiding soil improvement and fertilizers plants grow less vigorously, they remain lower, and do not need staking; nor do they spread as quickly and need replanting so often. Increasingly gardeners are learning to work with their plant material to realize their ideas rather than simply exploiting it for short-term

gains. This in turn introduces a deeper meaning to their efforts and offers greater scope for communication and expression.

The schemes of Heiner Luz (*see pp.41–3*) are at the cutting edge of this thinking. Although Luz is designing on a large scale and for the public domain, the application of his ideas to a smaller garden should be carefully considered. They offer a low-maintenance solution, with the possibility of clean modern lines that avoid the nostalgic associations of herbaceous border plantings, which to some may seem at odds with contemporary thinking and lifestyles.

Design Choices and Opportunities

Petra Pelz's simple bold design for a long narrow garden uses large clumps of *Miscanthus sinensis* grasses, now flowering, and trees as its structural elements. Shorter flowering perennials and bulbs for seasonal interest line the curving path, which leads to a small lawn and pavilion. The *Persicaria amplexicaulis* 'Alba' in the foreground is especially effective in late summer.

The location of a garden is fundamental to its design, as has already been mentioned in relation to culture, context, and climate. Beyond such constraints a garden could take on any number of forms. Some gardeners favour formality and order, while others choose curves and free expression. Minimalist gardeners will limit their planting palette to the bare essentials, while others will revel in the bounty of the plant world and overfill their beds and borders.

Your passions and taste will not only influence the way you arrange the design but also the plants you choose to grow. The design rules that stipulate harmonies and contrasts, rhythms and patterns, and sophisticated colour associations count for nothing when you introduce your personal preferences into the equation. Knowing the rules and breaking them is what instils a sense of place and allows garden-making to aspire to a form of artistic expressionism.

The atmosphere you strive to develop in your garden should direct your choices, because in the end it will not be a particular plant or colour theme that matters as much as the overall feel of the space created. Moods can vary from tranquil and still to stimulating and even intimidating; the choice is yours to make and develop.

The opportunity offered by a garden to sculpt a private domain is open to anyone with access to a piece of ground. Physical limitations count for nothing once you free your mind and explore your requirements both functionally and emotionally.

The final result of your effort will be a complex blend of passions and pragmatism for not every plant you want to use will accept the conditions in your garden and not every location will offer an appropriate setting in which to realize your dreams. However, such limits spark inspiration and creativity, leading to infinite variations and modulations.

Design Constraints

Plants have evolved over millions of years to inhabit every conceivable environment on earth. At one extreme these may be simple algae and mosses and at the other giant forest trees. No matter where you garden there will be plants that can survive and even thrive. Much of gardening history is the tale of man's fight with nature; landscapes have been radically altered and artificial habitats created to enable exotic plants to succeed. Although with today's knowledge and techniques such artificiality is even easier to realize, increasing awareness of environmental issues inexorably pulls gardeners in the opposite direction.

Today's more natural approach to gardening encourages the growth of plants that will succeed in the conditions available in your garden. This does not mean that you have to give up and hand the land back to wild nature. Shelterbelts should still be considered, to tame excessive winds, and soils might be improved to encourage establishment.of young plants. It is the

BELOW In the Jac. P Thijsse park in Amstelveen, The Netherlands, native plants which have adapted to the inhospitable, acidic soils of the region are grown in a highly structured and aesthetically pleasing design. Here sun-loving, yellow-flowering bog asphodel (*Narthecium ossifragum*) still looks attractive in autumn against a background of shade-tolerant royal ferns (*Osmunda regalis*).

ABOVE Sun-lovers from different countries have here combined to form an eye-catching display. Silver-leaved *Stachys byzantina* comes from Turkey, south-western Asia, and Iran, *Dianthus carthusianorum* originates in the European Alps, while the purple allium is native to Turkestan.

excesses of the past that are becoming increasingly taboo: insecticides, fertilizers, and resorting to watering during hot summer weather. The traditional herbaceous border with its regime of soil improvement resulting in excessive plant growth, which requires continuous staking, is clearly no longer in favour, nor is the use of plants that in such conditions either outgrow their allotted space or exhaust themselves and need replanting every few years.

Around the globe habitats exist that have similar characteristics, and the plants that grow there have evolved to exploit each particular combination of exposure, moisture level, light level, and soil type. Within a garden, you can bring together plants from different parts of the world that grow in similar habitats and combine them into planting schemes that are appropriate to the available conditions. Such plants will have a natural compatibility even though they are not found growing together in nature.

By carefully selecting plants that have adapted to existing garden conditions, you can save yourself and the environment a great

LEFT A sunny courtyard is a suitable setting for sun-loving *Nepeta racemosa* 'Walker's Low', *Salvia nemorosa*, and pink valerian (*Centranthus ruber*).

BELOW FAR LEFT *Libertia peregrinans* and *Thymus longicaulis* here thrive in the challenging conditions to be found in Beth Chatto's gravel garden.

BELOW LEFT Vigorous *Aster trinervius* subsp. *ageratoides* var. *yezoensis* (syn. *A. ageratoides*) makes effective groundcover in the dry shade beneath trees.

BELOW Beth Chatto turned a sun-baked car park in Essex, England, into a colourful gravel garden as an experiment in gardening in tune with existing conditions. The yellow asphodels (*Asphodeline lutea*) clearly revel in the parched, gravelly soil.

deal of stress and energy. Plants naturally grow healthily, resist disease, and tend to share characteristics that harmonize them with their neighbours both aesthetically as well as in terms of their competitiveness, resulting in balanced plant communities. With every plant in a scheme reacting in the same way to the ambient conditions, interventions are reduced and the same maintenance regimes can be applied to them all at the same time. For example, being able to cut all the plants down in one go rather than having to deal with them individually saves time, and when public planting schemes are involved this can have a big impact on maintenance costs.

SOIL TYPES AND GARDEN HABITATS

The structure of soil can vary from sandy, light, and free draining to thick, heavy clay, which becomes saturated in winter and can be baked hard in summer. Neither extreme is ideal. Another crucial component of soil is humus, which controls its fertility as well as its porosity and water-holding capacity. Humus is partially decayed organic material and is alive with a complex community of micro-organisms. Both sandy and clay soils can be improved by the addition of composted garden waste, leaf mould, or manure, which will increase the amount of humus present and so benefit plant growth. The addition of sand and grit to clay soils will further improve their porosity and provide conditions suitable for a wider range of plants to be grown than in unimproved soil.

Sandy soils dry out quickly and so are suitable for drought-tolerant plants. The typical Mediterranean flora is well adapted to these types of soils when they occur in open sunny situations. When gravel is spread over the soil surface to help retain moisture, gardens with a distinctive open character can be developed, with tough-leaved, wiry subshrubs such as lavender, perovskia, phlomis, rosemary, rue, hyssop, and thyme,

Native to Columbia and south Brazil *Gunnera manicata* is found growing along the banks of rocky streams. Its habitat is characterized by fog and almost daily rainfall. The more moisture gunnera receives, the more dramatic its huge leaves become. Shelter, fertile soil, and winter protection are prerequisites for its successful cultivation in temperate climates.

providing the permanent structure for a planting scheme incorporating such perennials as acanthus, achillea, artemisia, echium, euphorbia, kniphofia, nepeta, salvia, and sedums. Many bulbs thrive in such open situations, especially when accompanied by the milder conditions near the coast. Allium, asphodelus, dierama, eremurus, gladiolus, tulbaghia, and tulips are just some of so many that could be used to develop dramatic planting themes in such places.

Members of the pea family are also successful in sandy soils, because the presence of nitrogen-fixing bacteria within nodules on their root systems enables them to overcome the low nutrient levels typical of such soils. Lupins being so easily grown from seed are therefore an obvious choice for creating wide drifts of early summer colour. Perennial members of the sweet pea family such as climbing *Lathyrus grandiflorus* and

clump-forming *L. vernus* also offer a range of possible planting combinations.

Many of the grasses are adapted to grow in sandy soils. Sand dunes are the home of *Leymus arenarius* and *Ammophila arenaria*, which would normally be excluded from conventional garden borders, where they spread aggressively. However, these and other grasses such as eragrostis, festuca, helictotrichon, pennisetum, and numerous species of stipa could all be used to stabilize loose sandy soils within a garden. In coastal locations they look appropriate where, tossed by the wind, they bring movement and drama to the gardening scene.

Where sandy soils occur in combination with shade there are fewer plants that will thrive. Dry shade in particular, whether or not as the result of the sandy soil or of competition from surface-rooting trees, is one of the gardener's greatest challenges. Trial and error will be the only way to identify what will grow in any situation, although few plants establish well unless given a pocket of good soil to start with and some cosseting while they attempt to become established. The grass *Deschampsia cespitosa* will sometimes succeed in dry shade, and woodrushes (*Luzula*) are almost guaranteed to work. Other common groundcover plants that often cope with such conditions include epimediums, omphalodes, common ivy, and even tough ferns such as *Dryopteris filix-mas*.

When planting in such difficult conditions it is best to identify what grows and use it extensively, rather than attempting planting combinations that are more ambitious. However, endless drifts of woodrushes or epimediums can easily become monotonous. One way to introduce variety is to use plants that are often termed invasive and unsuitable for small gardens. Growing under stress, their aggressive character is tamed, yet they survive and produce an effective show. Try *Aster macrophyllus*, for example, which bears large, heart-shaped leaves and open heads of starry, lilac-tinted flowers in late summer through to autumn. Another good choice might be *Trachystemon orientalis*, whose huge, rough-textured leaves form attractive groundcover most of the year in sun or shade. It spreads quickly both at the root and by seeding around, and in spring it has a fleeting display of spidery, lilac-blue flowers. Likewise, *Lysimachia ciliata* eventually becomes a problem in a conventional border, yet in dry shade it springs up here and there bringing variety with its simple foliage and nodding yellow flowers in mid-summer.

Heavier clay soils are generally richer in nutrients and can support a far wider range of perennials than sandy ones. The limiting factor is often the poor soil structure leading to waterlogging in winter and parched, cracked conditions in dry summers. Many grasses and plants associated with the North American prairie accept these conditions, making this soil type ideal for experimenting with the recent trend for naturalistic gardens.

The majority of perennials accept a wide range of soil types from acidic to strongly alkaline, but in some cases the soil's pH will impose limitation on what may be grown. Various species of lilies, trilliums, gentians, and some ferns, for example, need acidic soil.

There is an exciting range of plants specifically adapted to damp and even saturated soils, not to mentions those that grow in water either along its margins or totally submerged. Their character is very different from drought-tolerant species. Typically they are lush growing with broad leaves, offering the opportunity to create bold planting schemes based on dramatic foliage contrasts. Gunneras with leaves up to 1m (3ft) wide are one of the largest perennials you may be able to grow, and their size in a garden is nearly always a reflection of the availability of soil moisture. Other moisture-lovers include rodgersias, darmeras, and skunk cabbages (*Lysichiton*). Colour is far from absent in the bog garden when wide drifts of spring-flowering primulas or summer-flowering astilbes are grown, while in autumn rich tints develop in the fronds of ferns.

Candelabra primulas and skunk cabbages (*Lysichiton americanus*) flourish in the permanently moist conditions found in the Norfolk Broads, England.

SETTINGS

The woodland edge is the natural habitat of many popular garden plants. This particular environment has a varying amount of shade, avoids being excessively dry, and offers shelter to the plants that it nurtures. In many ways suburban gardens provide similar conditions when shade is cast by neighbouring trees, walls, and buildings. However the informality of the woodland edge is not always an appropriate format in a garden situation, especially when it is adjacent to modern buildings. Simple, even minimalistic planting generally works better in such situations, and upright ornamental grasses seem one of the very best options.

While growing conditions place limitations on what perennials may be cultivated, a garden's location in terms of buildings, the countryside, its proximity to the coast, and any number of other cultural and contextual influences impose further constraints on what seems right and what looks out of place. Tom Stuart-Smith's design for Broughton Grange in Somerset, England, is aligned with various patterns and focal points in the surrounding

landscape (*see pp.58–59*). The wash of perennials on its terraces creates a setting from which to view the dramatic rolling countryside beyond. Both the garden and the surrounding fields are man-made but with different functions in mind, and the planting seeks to emphasize this by the use of exotics on the one hand and naturalistic imagery on the other.

The very different garden at Sleightholmedale Lodge on a dramatic slope in North Yorkshire, England, is both conventional and quite unusual (*see p.58*). This family garden was made in the 1960s and has changed very little since then. The decision to make the double border rise up the valley side, rather than follow a horizontal contour, brings the surrounding landscape into dramatic focus. When viewed from above the planting plunges away, and it is necessary to climb to reach its top. The plants are old-fashioned cultivars that nobody knows the names of any more, yet they have survived the extreme conditions of the site. The dramatic clumps of purple lythrums that dominate in summer were collected years ago

The reasons plants are chosen for locations can vary. *Calamagrostis* x *acutiflora* 'Karl Foerster' has been used (*left*) to form a visual link with the dramatic skyline of Chicago, while the newly planted border (*right*) on the roof of London's National Theatre seems to be purely an aesthetic exercise in complementary and contrasting shapes as well as textures.

RIGHT The designer Jacqueline van der Kloet has filled these borders with a homogeneous mix of the same perennials and ornamental grasses such as *Stipa tenuissima* (*in the foreground and right*) and *Calamagrostis* x *acutiflora* (*in the centre*). The planting is in scale with the setting and alternates with areas of open lawn throughout the extensive site of this office complex in Amsterdam.

ABOVE *Lythrum salicaria* dominates the foreground of the precipitous double border at Sleightholmedale Lodge, England.

from the banks of a nearby river. The orange crocosmia has refused to be eliminated and has now become an integral part of this spectacular, idiosyncratic border.

Such planting choices are subjective, and everyone has their limits. For example, a wonderful gravel garden repleat with cacti and succulents surrounded by rolling green English countryside might jar horribly with its setting to many people.

MAINTENANCE

Another constraint that is too often overlooked by enthusiastic gardeners is the availability of labour to maintain their planting schemes. Changing lifestyles and the onset of old age may make what was once acceptable no longer feasible in the garden. When tasks such as weeding, watering, and staking need to be reduced, the key to success may be close planting of ground cover and growing plants hard without overfeeding them. However, some jobs cannot be avoided. For example, perennials normally need cutting down and their dead material carrying away in winter or early spring. In a small garden, three or four afternoons' work in late winter should be sufficient to see the dead top-growth removed and the borders made ready for the new year. This is something you should be able to undertake at a relatively quiet time of the year.

RIGHT The transition from the surrounding farmland to the garden at Lady Farm, Somerset, England, has been carefully managed by sowing the field on the left with a wildflower and grass mixture; on the right the garden begins with a simple naturalistic scheme of *Deschampsia cespitosa* grasses interplanted with *Phlomis russeliana*.

Stylistic Expression

The clothes you wear, the car you drive, your home, and your choice of partner are all expressions of who you are and what you consider important and relevant in life. Order or chaos, freedom or discipline, attention to detail or interest in the wider picture are all terms that may be applied to different people and their lifestyles. Your garden is yet another expression of this.

The growing interest in gardening and garden design in recent decades has a number of causes. At a practical level it represents a need for space in an ever-busier and crowded society. Homes are often small and any available outdoor space offers an opportunity to expand the living area – at least at the times of the year you can use it. When viewed through a window or connected by a sliding glass door, the garden can be coordinated with the interior furnishings to become an "outdoor room".

However, a stronger urge may well underpin many attempts to create gardens: the need to take control and express individuality in a world where increasingly this is submerged in globalization. The garden becomes an Arcadia, the one place left you have complete control to indulge your passions and assert your freedoms. If any trends in garden design are to be named, this need for self-expression underpins them all, and it promises an exciting future for garden art and artists.

RIGHT The central axis is a recurring theme in landscape and garden design – it brings order, balance, and calm. Here in Germany, an axial water tank defines this space and is surrounded by massed *Alchemilla mollis*.

BELOW Christopher Lloyd's garden at Great Dixter, Sussex, England, is one man's expression of his approach to planting. The justly famous long border combines shrubs, perennials, bulbs, and annuals in ways that are uniquely his own.

CONTROL AND ORDER

For some people a preference for a straight line rather than a curve sums up their approach to garden design. An inclination for a formal design is a choice for organization, logic, and balance in your surroundings. The formally laid-out garden has a long history and continues to this day to win favour. In its simplest form a chequerboard of square beds separated by straight paths can become the logical layout for a vegetable garden or the flowerbeds in a botanic garden. Depictions of the medieval *hortus conclusus* show such designs with square beds for flowers being contained by high protective walls.

ABOVE Uncompromising in their arrangement, the mirror borders at Bramdean House, Hampshire, England, lead straight out of the house and up a gentle slope. In early summer clumps of catmint (*Nepeta*) are repeated along the length and either side of the central path.

LEFT This stepped water rill gently flows towards the dining room of Colemore House in Hampshire, England. On either side, the planting of *Salvia nemorosa* and *Alchemilla mollis* is formally arranged and repeated along its length.

The Islamic garden with its stylized depiction of heaven on earth includes rivers ordered into straight rills or canals crossing a central point to divide the space into equal proportions. In the Renaissance, man's assertion over nature was depicted in formal gardens centred on a villa. In northern Europe this representational style subsequently exploded into the formal designs for palace gardens, parks, and even entire cities. In every case the central axis is the fulcrum. The straight line introduces control and order, and with this comes a sense of stability, balance, and peace to the design.

The formal style when applied to planting likewise introduces a sense of control and order to a garden space. Frequently such designs are focused on the house or buildings, with plants lining paths that lead from doors and entrances towards the boundaries. When plants are massed together, set out in rows, or placed at regular intervals they lose their individuality and become components of a larger picture. The tulip, for example, is an elegant simple flower when seen up close and when used in discrete planting associations in a garden. When the same plant is massed together on a traffic island or in a park flowerbed, it becomes just one small part of a wide splash of colour. Your response to a plant can therefore vary not only through the associations you attach to it, its colour, and form, but also in the ways that you decide to use and group it.

Just five species of perennials have been used to create this atmospheric garden. These include *Actaea simplex*, *Salvia nemorosa*, *Thalictrum rochebruneanum*, and a bamboo, each planted in separate blocks. *Alchemilla mollis* fills the space beneath a peristyle of pollarded *Catalpa bignonioides* trees.

THE MINIMALIST APPROACH

Formal planting tends to use a limited palette of plants, which are repeated and massed to create a bold and harmonious effect. A more recent variation on the idea is to be found in the simplified planting schemes associated with contemporary urban landscape architecture. The spin-off from this in the domestic arena is the so-called Minimalist garden, which became an internationally fashionable in the 1990s.

Minimalism has two primary foci: the logical organization of functional space, and a preoccupation with the elimination of clutter and superfluous detail. Plants in the Minimalist garden must function within these strict parameters. Minimalism arose as an architectural concept and in its application has many similarities with other branches of three-dimensional art where space, as much as the objects that surround it, is emphasized and manipulated.

In the so-called Minimalist garden plants are used either as the building blocks that contain outdoor spaces or to carpet these areas. Trees, hedges, and tall-growing perennials form the three-dimensional framework and groundcover plants cover the surfaces. Interestingly, the Minimalist approach tends to use the same plants en masse and rarely mixes them or brings them together in any form of association that might draw attention to contrasts of texture or form at an individual level, for example. Emphasis on such detail seems to be confined to specimen plants isolated from others, such as the lone tree or cactus set in a sea of paving.

A rather brutal aspect to this sort of design approach is that it seems to want to deny the glorious diversity and subtlety of the plant kingdom. To achieve its aesthetic aim, the smallest range of plants is chosen in what seems to be an attempt to deny any interference that might come about through plant association and interplay. Woolly romantic impressions are simply out of the question.

Because of its lack of associations and identity, Minimalist planting therefore seems more appropriate for public spaces rather than private gardens. It also offers the benefit of a simplified maintenance regime. In America, the design team of James van Sweden and Wolfgang Oehme has created a planting style using wide drifts of the same plants, such as sedums or grasses, as a direct response to the poor levels of maintenance available in public green spaces in that country. However, they include a wider palette of plants than in a strict Minimalistic style, as associations with the grass prairies of their homeland underpin their design philosophy.

At ground level, sheets of perennials or low-growing shrubs are often selected in Minimalist-style gardens to carpet open spaces; but why? Since people are unlikely to walk on a bed of *Salvia nemorosa* or *Sedum telephium* one reason could be to control movement and circulation through the garden. However, a sheet of water or even rough gravel would do the same job. More likely, the Minimalist designer wishes to introduce texture or colour in order to contrast the planting with adjacent hard surfaces such as walls of glass, marble, or concrete. The monolithic forms of many modern buildings seem to be enhanced by bold expanses of wiry or woolly plant material, especially when the plants look good all year round. Old-fashioned ivy, hardy geraniums, and other traditional groundcover plants are still popular choices, but the palette has been extended recently to include perennial grasses, sedges, salvias, and sedums – all plants that lend themselves to being grown side by side to create a uniform mass.

ABOVE *Rudbeckia maxima* looks good when forming a simple architectural block of planting.

BELOW Attention is drawn to this garden pavilion by a colourful carpet of *Salvia nemorosa* 'Ostfriesland'.

In flower, many of these newer choices can alter the feel of the spaces they occupy as well as highlight seasonal changes.

Plants also have bulk, and when this is associated with an upright form they can be grouped together to create architectural blocks. Such plants when tall and narrow become the garden's walls and screens; when low and wide, its terraces and platforms. Ornamental grasses are exciting to use in this way, especially those that grow tall and upright throughout the summer and then die down in winter, such as miscanthus, calamagrostis, and the see-through veils of molinias. Unlike traditional hedging plants, these are constantly altering the garden's architecture as they grow. In spring the space is open, perhaps crisscrossed with lines of greenery, but by late summer sight-lines have been blocked and more intimate garden spaces created, possibly offering differing moods and changed experiences.

Flower colour, although transient, may also be the reason behind a plant being introduced. Colour has a powerful effect on your mood and can be used to alter your perceptions of the spaces in which you find yourself. The green room is supposed to sooth, and a courtyard filled with blood red salvias will probably make you want to pass through it quickly.

The current emphasis in garden design on form and texture, where colour is allowed to take care of itself, fails to recognize just how powerfully people react to it. In the Minimalist garden, colour will always have been carefully taken into consideration, if only because each plant is going to be repeated so many times in the same space and therefore will dominate it.

Because every aspect of a plant's character – size, form, texture, and colour – needs to be taken into account before it is included in the final design in a Minimalist-style garden, the results of such a approach can be extremely powerful. However, when planting is simplified to this extent, it can all too soon become monotonous and boring. Therefore, for some people, planting design needs to include an emotional element, which brings into play associations not just of size, form, texture, and colour but also of personal and private memories, thoughts, and aspirations. In other words, when you pull out all the stops, planting design can become a potent means of self-expression filled with passion and excitement.

ABOVE This mass planting of *Pycnanthemum muticum* is completely in tune with the open view beyond. This plant needs moist soil to thrive, as here in its native North America.

RIGHT Attention is drawn to an outdoor sitting area at Arlanda airport, Stockholm, in a design by Ulf Nordfjell. The flight of stairs leading to it is exaggerated and given great impact by rows of *Sedum kamtschaticum* var. *floriferum* 'Weihenstephaner Gold'.

LEFT A band of *Anemanthele lessoniana* (syn. *Stipa arundinacea*) makes a bold contrast with a smooth, plain-coloured wall in the background.

INFORMALITY

The choice between a formal or informal planting style may be intuitive. Both styles are equally assertive, and both can be incorporated into a single garden's design when you want to contrast attitudes about control and order with ideas of free expression, wild nature, or chaos theory. Each planting style may also suit different settings with the tidy formal design being used in the public domain of a front garden, for example, and a free informal style introduced in private or hidden areas of the garden.

An informal planting style tends to draw attention to plants as individuals. The manner in which they are combined might range from the randomness of flowers in a meadow to the purposeful, refined associations of the herbaceous border. In every case, the plants themselves are crucial to the emotional reactions and messages such schemes are expected to evoke. This is in contrast with formal planting, where the order and repetition serve to define a layout, focus attention on a building, or overwhelm through their scale and control over natural forces.

ABOVE Curving paths invite you to follow and find out what lies beyond in these in borders that have yet to reach their peak of flowering. Here in early summer, repetitive planting of *Allium hollandicum* creates a feeling of unity.

Informal schemes infer intimacy and attempt to draw you into their detail. Paths are sinuous, hidden depths infer mystery, and the plants chosen may have symbolic significance, evoking feelings of nostalgia and history. The English cottage-garden style is the embodiment of all of this.

In truth, cottagers in the 19th century grew food in their gardens to survive and medicinal plants to use as home remedies; their circumstances were generally harsh and their gardens functional. However, nostalgic images of rustic simplicity have been projected on to such small-scale country gardens and have developed into the romantic cottage-garden style. Plants are supposedly arranged randomly, their colours allowed to mix freely, and when a domestic use can be attributed to them – such as herbal, culinary, or dyeing – they reinforce the fantasy world that is being recreated.

The influential British garden designer Gertrude Jekyll was instrumental in building the nostalgia surrounding the cottage-garden style. Clearly under its influence herself, she developed an informal way of planting in which groups of plants drifted into one another in aesthetically contrived combinations with colour harmonies and contrasts carefully orchestrated. Her planting was clearly an attempt to seduce her audience to overpower their senses and evoke images of pastoral beauty with her blends of simple cottage-garden flowers.

BELOW Informal planting in a symmetrical layout around the old fountain is Piet Oudolf's theme in the Walled Garden at Scampston Hall. Accents of sesleria and phlomis stand out in a design dominated by monarda and catmint (*Nepeta*).

Belgium cobblestones add to the informal lines at Bury Court, England in borders filled with sun-loving perennials such as catmint (*Nepeta*), salvias, and veronicas.

What brought Gertrude Jekyll universal acclaim was her collaboration with the architect Edwin Lutyens, who designed formal settings in which her informal style of planting was placed. It was a formula that appealed to people of all tastes, allowing the romance of the countryside to enter a neat world of control and order.

Informal planting within an organized, hard-edged setting is just as popular today, even though modern designers have started to develop a different palette of plants, which require less intensive maintenance or invoke a different set of associations. Piet Oudolf's planting of sun-loving perennials in the central section of his design for the old vegetable garden at Scampston Hall (*top right*) evokes the cottage-garden style. An informal mixture of medium-height plants creates a wavy field of colour, yet the plants are growing in a series of regularly arranged

beds. This central section of the design is positioned within a larger design of formal spaces; some are filled with plants and others not. Here the informal cottage-garden style is being used as a stylistic reference and placed in a context where it makes a bold contrasting statement against older and more contemporary planting theories.

Wild plants grow in patterns that reflect their interrelationships in their natural habitats. What appears as random and informal is in fact the result of complex evolution. Some plants spread sideways and suppress their neighbours; others are slim and airy, finding space and light without overwhelming neighbouring, lower-growing species. Some wild plants spread underground while others shed their seed far and wide. Outside observers register such distribution patterns and may be inspired to reproduce them in their own gardens.

RIGHT The rolling field of perennial colour in front of the greenhouse at Scampston Hall includes the tall yellow flowers of *Rudbeckia maxima* in the centre, which make an eye-catching feature.

BELOW The shape of the borders and the mounds of plants within them reflect the patterns to be found in the undulating hills beyond in this country garden, which has been designed by Tom Stuart-Smith at Brockhampton Cottage, Herefordshire, England.

THE GERMAN ECOLOGICAL APPROACH

A considerable amount of attention has been focused on the ecological aspect of informal planting in Germany. The emphasis has not been to recreate a natural plant community in a garden but rather to find groups of compatible plants that are perfectly suited to the available growing conditions. Research undertaken by Professor Richard Hansen at the trial ground Weihenstephan near Munich began by defining garden situations into habitats that could be related to those that

exist in nature: woodland, woodland edge, open ground, rock garden, border, water's edge and marsh, and water.

He split perennials into two main groups, which had as much to do with their management requirements in a garden as to their origins. Border perennials are the traditional components of the herbaceous border; they are the product of years of breeding and selection by gardeners and include such favourites as irises, delphiniums, and phlox. They need an

LEFT At the Hermannshof trial garden in Weinheim, Germany, an area has been planted with a mixture of North American prairie plants that reach a peak of flowering in late summer. However, here in early summer *Penstemon digitalis* 'Husker Red' dominates among plants also in flower, which include the disease-resistant *Monarda menthifolia* in the foreground.

BELOW This early summer scheme includes *Salvia nemorosa*, *S. sclarea* var. *turkestanica*, *Achillea* 'Coronation Gold', and in the centre *Phlomis russeliana*. All plants require full sun and perfect drainage to thrive.

North American prairie, such as rudbeckias, boltonias, and solidagos. Numerous woodland perennials have a wild character, as do ferns and grasses. Such plants tend to colonize the soil quickly and overwhelm any traditional border perennials growing nearby. Planting schemes that mix Hansen's two groups of perennials should therefore be avoided.

When planting schemes composed of only wild perennials are used, they tend to find a state of equilibrium over time and therefore the plants should not be divided regularly and the soil they grow in should not be disturbed. Once established, such beds require far less maintenance, and it is suggested that the plants they contain harmonize especially well through shared characteristics born through their adaptation to similar habitats. Perennials with a wild character are ideal for informal planting schemes, where they are left alone to develop a harmonious balance with one another.

Hansen has further refined his ideas to assign to different plants his so-called sociability index. This ranges from I for plants that should be used singly or in small groups, II for planting groups of 3–10, III for larger

open soil structure, which is regularly cultivated and fed, as is typically found in a flowerbed. They prefer open sunny conditions and do not handle competition from neighbouring plants particularly well.

In contrast, Hansen's wild perennials are true species both native and exotic or their selections which still retain their wild character. Many of the smaller-flowered asters, as opposed to the cultivars of *Aster novae-angliae* and *A. novi-belgii*, fall into this group, as do other perennials associated with the

ABOVE Richard Hansen's work on perennials have made the trial gardens at Weihenstephan in Freising, Germany, famous. In one demonstration bed for an open sunny aspect is a mixture of medium- to low-growing perennials including mounds of *Euphorbia seguieriana*, evergreen yuccas, grasses, including *Stipa gigantea, Helictotrichon sempervirens*, and *Festuca mairei*, subshrubs such as perovskia and lavenders, together with a host of aromatic herbs including nepeta, calamintha, stachys, and salvia. The plants are repeated and grouped according to their assigned sociability indices.

LEFT Matching plants of equal vigour is the key to creating a balanced, low-maintenance community. Here *Chamerion angustifolium* 'Album', a garden form of rosebay willowherb, colonizes successfully with *Lysimachia ciliata* – a similarly competitive plant.

groups of 10–20 plants, and IV for larger patches, through to V for extensive planting for very large areas. Here he is concerned with the way plants should be repeated through a scheme with a few specimen plants being combined with different-sized groups of medium- and small-growing plants in a natural manner.

Solitary plants from group I include upright grasses such as molinias and panicums, large clumps of *Macleaya cordata* and *Persicaria polymorpha*, and upright perennials such as *Salvia haematodes* and verbascums. Asters and many familiar daisies are placed in groups II and III, while excellent groundcover species for large areas include *Geranium endressii* and *G. macrorrhizum*, *Lysimachia punctata*, various sedums and *Tiarella cordifolia*.

Hansen's lists make fascinating reading as they combine the results of experiments that have evaluated ease of maintenance with aesthetic judgments. His rules might not be followed slavishly, yet they do highlight the weaknesses inherent in many planting schemes, especially those encountered at garden shows, which need to impress their visitors for only a short period.

LEFT The spirit of the American prairie has been evoked by Piet Oudolf, who chose coneflowers (*Echinacea purpurea* 'Rubinglow'), *Eryngium yuccifolium*, and the ornamental grass *Molinia caerulea*. Drifts of *Allium senescens* subsp. *montanum* 'Summer Beauty' enrich the display, but are not native; nor need they be in this naturalistic scheme to be found in downtown Chicago.

RIGHT Piet Oudolf combines plants to emphasize their individual characteristics, as can be seen here in this subtle association of *Limonium platyphyllum* (syn. *L. latifolium*) and *Origanum laevigatum* 'Herrenhausen'.

NATURALISTIC PLANTING

An informal style of planting which has become popular in recent years has been termed naturalistic. In truth the style is far removed from anything to be found in nature, but in spirit it emulates natural associations and uses them to engage our senses and draw the onlooker into subtle combinations of natural forms and processes.

The pragmatic German system of grouping perennials based on garden habitat and sociability, however, comes a lot nearer to emulating nature, even though its fundamental aim is to create attractive, cost-effective solutions for public green space while reserving border perennials for high-maintenance planting schemes in close proximity to homes and buildings.

Both styles of planting are capable of dramatic visual impact, but the naturalistic approach attempts to go further artistically and expressively. Typically it uses a more complex mix of perennials, and it will happily break the rule of not combining wild and border perennials when aesthetics demand.

The Dutch designer Piet Oudolf is a leading exponent of the naturalistic style, but others such as Urs Walser and Petra Pelz in Germany, Wolfgang Oehme and James van Sweden in the USA, Ulf Nordfjell in Sweden, and Tom Stuart-Smith and Dan Pearson in England have all developed their own variations on the theme. What sets this style of informal planting apart is the inclusion in garden borders of Professor Hansen's wild perennials as well as border perennials that exhibit wild characteristics. These designers are in search of perennials with expressive characteristics in order to develop planting schemes in which the individual components can make dramatic contrasts with one another. Tall molinia grasses may for instance shoot high out of a lake of frothy astrantia or edge a shoreline of boulderlike persicaria or asters, yet the plants all look as if they belong together as they share natural attributes.

The whole character of the plants used in naturalistic schemes is important and not just one feature such as their flower colour or leaf shape. The plants should show their

LEFT Subtle tints harmonize contrasting forms and textures in a scheme designed by Ulf Nordfjell in Sweden. The focus of attention is about to shift away from the tall *Eupatorium purpureum* and fading flowers of *Astrantia major* towards the dramatic foliage of *Actaea simplex* 'James Compton' and miscanthus grass ready to make an entrance stage right.

RIGHT Grasses seem crucial to schemes adopting the naturalistic style. Here *Miscanthus sinensis* 'Flammenmeer' grows in front of the vigorous wild form of *Phlox paniculata*.

personality from the moment they emerge above ground in spring through to senescence in autumn. The overall shape of the plant, its leaves, and the patterns they create establish its presence in a garden. Typically flowers are smaller and simpler than those of more traditional border perennials, creating a lighter, more open impression. Ideally such perennials should hold on to their dead stems and seed heads to make dark-toned silhouettes that extend their season of interest through autumn and into winter. Such an approach, Piet Oudolf explained to me, emphasizes the individual characteristics of the perennials through the associations and settings in which they are placed.

Ornamental grasses feature regularly in these naturalistic schemes. Not only do they possess distinctive forms that suggest many possible combinations with other perennials

but they also seem to radiate naturalness through their strong associations with countryside, the open field, or prairie.

The choice of plants and the way they are brought together create the signature of the different designers currently working in a naturalistic style of planting. Some may use a restricted palette and arrange the plants in wide, sweeping drifts that equate quite closely to the sociability indices that might be applied to them in Germany. Other naturalistic designers create more complex schemes with various sized groupings contrasting and harmonizing with one another. At the other end of the spectrum, plants may be used in a seemingly random mix to simulate the jumble of a wild stretch of countryside.

In all of the examples I have seen of this style the individual locations have had a

FOLLOWING PAGES Low-angled light brings this dreamlike scheme to life and accentuates the dramatic presence of white-flowered *Persicaria polymorpha* in the background. The border seems to melt into the landscape beyond at Bury Court, Hampshire, England.

marked influence on the ways the plants have been used. Piet Oudolf's design for the Dream Park in Enköping, Sweden, for example, centres on a wide meandering river of blue *Salvia nemorosa* cultivars, which flows down to the bank of the adjoining river. At Brockhampton Cottage in Herefordshire Tom Stuart-Smith has created flowing harmonious borders that reach out to the undulating countryside that dominates the location.

His design for the walled garden at Broughton Grange (*above*) is complex, bringing together the opposing traditions of the *hortus conclusus* (the medieval garden with neatly ordered flowerbeds protected by high walls) and walled-garden paradises on the one hand with gardens that merge seamlessly into their surrounding landscapes on the other. Paths, a water channel, and stairs define the garden's internal structure as do its broad oblong terraces, but within these guidelines smaller paths meander between the perennials, the patterns of which make clear references to the hills and fields beyond.

Within the confines of traditional walled gardens, Christopher Bradley-Hole adopts neat-edged flowerbeds as the ground plan for his seemingly random plantings. His perennial plantings are conceived as a total entity, and not as a series of separate beds as in a botanic garden; they create an all-embracing image through which you can walk and lose yourself. Another place for a stroll is the public park on the Chicago waterfront, which was planted by Piet Oudolf. Its enclosing hedges mimic the form of a walled garden, yet the scale of the surrounding skyscrapers rob it of any sense of isolation, placing it at the heart of the American Dream. Oudolf's use of many wild prairie perennials makes a direct connection with the endemic flora of this region and function to afford the garden the status of botanic garden within the State of Michigan.

What is common to all these design approaches is a desire not only to celebrate natural diversity and beauty but also to relate them to present-day needs and aspirations.

ABOVE Tom Stuart-Smith's own garden has spaces flooded with planting while other sections are left empty. In early summer *Stipa gigantea* plumes dance amid columns of yew (*Taxus baccata*) and foxgloves. The enclosures reflect the area's former use as a farmyard, and the planting – in form, colour, and pattern – makes strong associations with this heritage as well as the surrounding countryside.

RIGHT A water channel lined with common reed (*Phragmites australis*) forms the background to this public scheme where a curving river of *Persicaria amplexicaulis* 'Firetail' resists competition from yellow *Lysimachia ciliata*. Likewise the bold clumps of *Inula magnifica* and *Geranium psilostemon* have remained consistent sizes here over many years.

In his design for the old walled garden at Scampston Hall, Piet Oudolf has used a range of perennials, many with wild, naturalistic characteristics, within a formal framework. This juxtaposition of traditional and modern garden styles is refreshing, creating a contemporary garden in tune with the needs and aspirations of many gardeners. Maintenance is low, yet there is colour and spectacle. Seed heads form and are allowed to remain as part of the picture. *Nepeta racemosa* 'Walker's Low' furnishes some corners (*left*). *Monarda* 'Aquarius' creates mounds of vivid violet-purple, while the bright yellow-green grass *Sesleria autumnalis* and distinctive upright *Phlomis russeliana* (*top*), in a similar hue, bring vivid contrasts. The golden flower heads of *Deschampsia cespitosa* 'Goldtau' grass adds yet more naturalism to the scene (*above*).

COLOUR AND THE CREATION OF ATMOSPHERE

The way you react to the atmosphere of a place influences your mood. This in turn affects your desire to linger and enjoy the surroundings or move on in search of something more appealing. The feeling of a garden in which everything is in balance will be soothing. Formal gardens with their elements arranged in symmetrical patterns and planting schemes comprising a harmonious mix of similar forms or colours will settle your mood and be a tranquil, peaceful haven. The opposite is true when asymmetry and contrast dominate. Your mood may be lifted if you find the atmosphere stimulating, but not if it appears threatening. Should either arrangement be taken to excess the results become boring and lose the desired effect.

Sometimes, however, planting schemes are created not to please but rather to impress. Formal planting on the scale of Versailles was made to assert the French king's dominance, while the flashy display of colour at the entrance to a corporate headquarters may be there to affirm the company's presence and to impress visitors.

Most of the time gardens are created to present a friendly face to the world and provide a refuge. Planting should consist of an interplay of harmonies and contrasts in rhythms and patterns that engage the senses and manipulate moods. Sometimes the need will be for peace and a place to think and dream; at others you may desire to surprise and entertain. In my own garden I have created a tiny "room" with walls of tall grasses, in which a long uncluttered pond is surrounded by a simple planting of dark-leaved ligularias mixed with tall clumps of vernonia (*above*). This is where I choose to sit and watch the patrolling dragonflies in summer. In spring, however, that part of the garden is filled with gaily coloured tulips to announce the arrival of that season to the outside world and to indulge my passion for this exotic group of plants.

Colour is the most potent of all aspects of plant growth to affect the atmosphere of a garden space. As with form, scale, and texture both harmonies and contrasts are possible, and in some cases single-colour themes may be implemented. How far down this road you venture is a matter of personal taste. Although the naturalistic style of planting places its emphasis on form, texture, and association, it cannot ignore colour, which plays a key role in creating contrasts

ABOVE LEFT Simple blue *Nepeta* 'Six Hills Giant' and nothing more brings calm and unity to this part of the garden at Cothay Manor, Somerset, England.

ABOVE *Ligularia dentata* 'Othello' and *Vernonia crinita* 'Mammuth' will flower together in late summer in this poolside planting, but now, together with tall grasses, they build an enclosure for quiet contemplation.

RIGHT Ulf Nordfjell has given this garden of light and dark, in Stockholm, a sense of control and order while remaining dynamic and interesting in all seasons. Here white-flowered *Anaphalis triplinervis* creates a background for purple, summer-flowering *Allium sphaerocephalon*.

and harmonies. However, colour is unlikely to be the starting point of the design.

There are two aspects to the application of colour in a garden design: the physical reaction it provokes and the associations it creates. Eyes react to the different wavelengths of colour and may be stimulated not only by what they currently focus on but also by what they have just been looking at. This was the skill of Gertrude Jekyll, whose famous colour border at her home, Munstead Wood, introduced colours in a sequence as the visitor walked its length. The silver section was long enough to saturate the eye before the yellow one, which appeared all the

more brighter as a consequence. This intensified through to red and orange, with the result that when the following section of silver and blue was reached its colours seem all the more concentrated. By understanding the physical properties of colour you too can draw attention to a particular colour in your own designs whenever this is deemed important, as Jekyll did so successfully.

Apart from a purely superficial liking for it, the reason you may wish to emphasize a colour in a planting design is the associations it generates and the powerful way you tend to react to it. Red is the colour of passion and heat; it is stimulating and draws you to it. A garden flooded with red is likely to stop you in your tracks. The drama of such an attack on the senses is unlikely to make you want to linger, but it will remain in your memory. Blue on the other hand is associated with the sea, ice, and clear skies. It implies distance and cool and is perceived as a fresh antidote to

ABOVE In this English mixed border, the *Catalpa bignonioides* 'Aurea' trees are cut down each spring to stimulate the formation of larger leaves. Together with flat-topped *Achillea filipendulina* 'Parker's Variety', golden *Carex elata* 'Aurea', and its brown-tinted relative *Carex comans*, a lively scheme is created and is guaranteed to lift the spirits.

BELOW Although blues can be difficult to combine, they have found harmony in the soft light often found in Sweden. The effect would quickly be destroyed in harsh sun.

ABOVE Nori and Sandra Pope have built their reputation on theories in which colours are united into schemes that intensify their impact rather than make contrasts with others. In high summer *Crocosmia* 'Lucifer' takes centre stage supported by red-toned foliage and flowers. Backlighting enhances the richness of the design.

RIGHT The gaiety of this unashamed celebration of summer colour is clearly appropriate as the path here leads to a swimming pool. Yellow *Genista aetnensis, Inula magnifica*, and daylilies contrast with bright red *Crocosmia* 'Lucifer' and rust-red *Helenium* 'Moerheim Beauty'. Such a dramatic scheme in a larger space, however, would quickly become visually tiring.

heavy, warmer tones. Pure blue is rare in the garden, and when it occurs it is worshipped, as in gentians, blue poppies, and some delphiniums. Blue is also blended with red in various degrees to make shades of mauve, violet, and indigo; alternatively, it may be diluted by green. When light intensities are low, blue is more effective because it radiates more light than warmer colours such as red and orange. In Scandinavian countries, smoky greys and blues register well in their soft light and have become an intrinsic part of their design culture.

Each and every colour has its associations: orange is exotic, the colour of cinnamon and terracotta; yellow is sunshine and spring daffodils in my mind; while purple is regal, rich colour to add depth to a planting scheme. White is quite different, being a mixture of all colours. On its own it quickly becomes monotonous, but it is the perfect foil to all other colours. However, the most common colour in every garden is green. Not only is this inseparable from images of nature and naturalness in our minds but it is also said to be psychologically the most restful of all colours.

The application of colour in garden design cannot be avoided even when it is only a blend of different shades of green. Its use for its own sake lacks any fantasy on the part of the gardener, but when its power is harnessed to manipulate the atmosphere of a garden area it becomes an important design tool.

ABOVE Green provides the antidote to the colours that may fill other parts of a garden at Scampston Hall, Yorkshire, England. *Molinia caerulea* subsp. *caerulea* 'Poul Petersen' has been planted in long drifts within this enclosed area intended for sitting and unwinding.

ABOVE This perfect circle of clover in the centre of a small wood is a powerful statement within a complex of more intricate experimental borders in the garden of the renowned Dutch landscape designer Mein Ruys.

RIGHT Upright *Panicum virgatum* provides the backdrop to this cosy enclosure scene.

LEFT The typical tropical look, here using bamboo (*Phyllostachys*) from China, the shrub *Nandina domestica* from central China and Japan, *Gunnera manicata* from Columbia through to southern Brazil, and Japanese hostas.

RIGHT Ron Herman's occidental-style garden in San Francisco symbolizes the Western view of the orient. Even the fallen bamboo leaves are part of the fantasy.

BELOW Inspired by the savannahlike parkland of one prairie region he visited, Cassian Schmidt, the director of the Hermannshof garden, Weinheim, created this border using the violet-blue daisy flowers of *Erigeron speciosus* 'Grandiflora', upright *Penstemon digitalis*, and yellow *Coreopsis grandiflora*.

FANTASY AND SYMBOLISM

Gardens may offer the space in which to escape reality and enter another world. In some cases this may lead to the desire to recreate an image or memory of an exotic place. The tropical look is one such manifestation for people living in cool climates. In this, large-leaved gunneras, rodgersias, and hostas as well as tall-growing grasses and bamboos are combined with frost tender perennials such as cannas, dahlias, bananas, and gingers to transport you to the tropical paradise of your dreams. Not many of these plants will truly grow in the places you wish to escape to, but mental associations enable you to overlook such inaccuracies.

Such escapism can take the form of an interest with a foreign culture and their distinctive garden style. This accounts for the popularity of Japanese and Chinese gardens in the West, together with the plants associated with them. Again grasses and bamboos feature strongly, as do ferns and

other primitive plants such as horsetails and mosses together with many plants endemic to such regions, including not only perennials but also shrubs and trees like rhododendrons and handkerchief trees (*Davidia involucrata*). In America the term "occidental" is now being used to describe an increasingly popular style of gardening that freely uses a mix of such oriental references.

Islamic traditions include gardens that symbolize paradise on earth – their walls creating the threshold between daily life and fantasy. Their watercourses, fountains, and plants are loaded with symbolism. Among the trees would be palms, oriental planes, and cypresses as well as the fruit trees mentioned in the Koran's description of paradise. Essential flowers include roses (loaded with symbolism since Persian times), opium poppies, anemones, violets, narcissus, lilies, and not-to-be-forgotten tulips (during the long period of Ottoman rule).

When gardeners become passionate about a particular country or group of plants they may go to extraordinary lengths to recreate an aspect of its natural habitat in their own gardens. Rock gardens that faithfully depict parts of the Swiss Alps, the Scottish Highlands, or the windswept limestone pavements of northern England have all been lovingly created and maintained by gardening enthusiasts; likewise, waterside retreats, marshes, and meadows have been formed.

In recent years the North American prairie has been a significant influence on designers. Its combination of tall grasses and perennials such as asters, echinaceas, eupatoriums, and rudbeckias has become central to the naturalistic style of planting. In Europe these prairie-style plantings are conceived for purely aesthetic reasons, while in America they have become associated with the drive to preserve a vanishing aspect of the native vegetation and cultural heritage.

ABOVE A planting scheme incorporating African red hot pokers (*Kniphofia*) in combination with red rocks and hummocks of brown sedges is suggestive of a hillside in South Africa yet this pragmatic steppe planting is to be found at Lady Farm in England.

RIGHT By introducing ornamental grasses buffeted by the wind along the banks of the Hudson River, James van Sweden and Wolfgang Oehme have brought references to the tall grass prairie – symbolic of America's cultural heritage – right to the heart of downtown Manhattan.

BELOW It is easy for Europeans to forget that many of their most popular garden plants are the wildflowers of Americans. On Spider Island at the Chicago Botanic Garden, for example, Michael van Valkenburgh has filled a tranquil retreat with indigenous wildflowers. Perennials include *Echinacea purpurea*, yellow *Rudbeckia hirta*, and asters as well as native grasses such as *Hystrix patula* and *Sporobolus heterolepis*.

ABOVE The heemparken in Amstelveen are famous for their stylish presentation of habitat-dependent wildflowers. Here in early summer the woodland floor is lit up by the yellow flowers of greater celandine (*Chelidonium majus*) beneath closely planted birches (*Betula pendula*).

PROMOTION AND COMMUNICATION

The notion of the garden as an outdoor exhibition space has a long tradition. Collections of plants, be these in botanic gardens or private gardens, both conserve the plants they contain for the future and facilitate education and scientific study. Conservation areas and native-plant gardens offer the same possibilities and may be used to promote ideas of conservation by presenting the plants in attractive settings. In The Netherlands the famous native-plant gardens (*heemparken*) help to educate people living in urban areas about their native flora and convince them of the need to protect it through highly seductive planting schemes. In such gardens many perennials become the stars, growing in wide informal drifts that bring washes of colour to the woodland floor or open heathlands. The heemparks, however,

BELOW In spring, around the lake at the *heemparken* at Amstelveen, majestic clumps of royal ferns (*Osmunda regalis*) emerge stiffly erect before uncurling like serpents and demanding attention from the park's visitors.

BOTTOM Sculptures by Elizabeth Frink reside on a small island in the lake of an English country garden. In early summer they gain even greater impact when the sculptures appear to be grazing on orange daylily flowers (*Hemerocallis*).

Nevertheless, through associations of colour or form they may still serve to highlight aspects of planting and enhance the ideas underpinning a design.

Yet planting alone has the ability to communicate ideas even though sometimes visitors may need help in the form of an explanation or sign. My own garden in Amsterdam is a celebration of the dynamic nature of perennials. In it, huge plants grow quickly in one summer so they radically alter their surroundings, but a visitor cannot understand this when they are there on only one day of the year. I remember seeing a large border in Sweden that lacked the refined

are not conservation areas as the native plants are used in carefully controlled combinations involving a great deal of maintenance in order to create a spectacular impact.

Gardens may also offer a setting for the display of art, which can function to create focal points within its design. In the past sculpture and built objects held significance and meaning for their contemporaries, but today they are seen primarily as decoration.

LEFT The gardens at Waltham Place have had a radical facelift in recent years. The formality of the Square Garden is now challenged by the serpentine box hedges and by borders filled with grasses and bold perennials such as the *Persicaria polymorpha* which is dominating here in early summer.

RIGHT The formal double borders at Waltham Place encourage visitors to think about the cultural context of the plants such as the euphorbias, thalictrums, and "weeds" that they now find growing there.

handling of colour that I associated with its designer. Apparently I had arrived too late, as its aim had been to show a subtle blending of unopened flower buds in its various forms of sedum, anaphalis, and solidago.

Concentration on a particular group of plants or a collection of one type of plant will have a considerable impact on any garden. Some gardeners adore hardy geraniums or hostas which leads to one impression. Others may be interested in lilies or ferns, which need various settings and consequently lead to different designs. In such ways gardens are personalized and used as a forum for self-expression and a celebration of the things you appreciate and love. Perhaps this is the most genuine form of stylistic expression.

The owners of Waltham Place in England are committed conservationists. Within the conventional framework of this old estate garden with its walled gardens and yew hedges they invited the Dutch garden designer Henk Gerritsen to create a planting scheme that communicated some of their radical ideas. The word weed suggests a plant in the wrong place, but who has the right to say where that is? The square garden with its

old redbrick walls and rose-clad pergola has seen the introduction of serpentine gravel beds filled with sun-loving grasses, perennials, and self-seeding annuals that challenge the formality of their setting. The low box hedges that would once have neatly edged beds of roses are now writhing serpents around the ankles of massive clumps of perennials such as *Persicaria polymorpha, Sanguisorba tenuifolia, Telekia speciosa*, and the massive umbels of the monocarpic *Peucedanum verticillare*.

The enormous yew hedges that previously backed the long double borders in front of the house have be clipped into unruly mounds. Along its length half-moon-shaped beds have been cut into the borders and backed by neat low hornbeam hedges. Within these gardens within gardens, vegetables are growing and running to seed. The parsnips throw up elegant yellow umbel flowers and act as climbing frames for bindweed – the last thing most gardeners expect to find in such a grand setting. The result of all this is both beautiful and breathtaking; with every step, planting conventions are challenged and this is precisely the aim of its owners and creator.

Themes and Seasonal Highlights

Plants including perennials serve various roles in garden design ranging from functional components of the skeletal structure to ephemeral incidents of decorative seasonal colour. Perennials such as *Eupatorium purpureum*, *Filipendula rubra* 'Venusta', *Helianthus microcephalus*, *Inula magnifica*, and *Persicaria polymorpha* grow into tall massive clumps that create bulk and structure within a planting scheme – as might equally well be provided by shrubs in a mixed border. Such plants, together with tall grasses and any perennials planted in bold architectural blocks, are the first group to be placed in any planting design.

Within the framework they create, other perennials can be arranged to introduce variations in form, texture, and importantly flower colour. This decorative element comprises the theme plants, which introduce the seasonal highlights.

Perennials are at their most invaluable in the garden when they are being used as theme plants. Their vast range of colours and forms offers endless possibilities for combination and artistic expression. Flowering in different seasons, they can be used to chart the annual cycle and produce seasonal highlights. It is in this role that the excitement and interest in gardening with perennials lies for most gardeners.

To be effective, theme plants need to be used in quantity and repeated within a garden space if they are going to have a real impact. A single aquilegia in spring makes a charming incident, but a garden where aquilegias pop up everywhere between other plants instantly gains the look and feel of a cottage garden through association and their seemingly random repetition across the whole area.

With careful planning a sequence of thematic plantings can be developed to span the whole gardening year, and it is this aspect of gardening with perennials that I shall be looking at in the second half of this book.

The damp soil adjacent to a natural watercourse provides ideal conditions for a bold thematic display of astilbes. In mid-summer *Astilbe chinensis* var. *davidii* in the background is combined with dark-toned *A.* 'Rotlicht' and other cultivars to create a colourful spectacle. Eventually seed heads form in complementary shades of brown and tan, and these continue to contribute to the garden scene for many months.

Introduction

Gardening is a process, sometimes with a beginning but never with an end. Your experiences can be as transient as the appearance of a rainbow over the horizon and the glint of frosted blades of grasses early on a winter's morning. Each day, week, and season brings changes to a garden, and as the years tick by plants mature, trees and shrubs grow larger, and even walls and buildings may enter or disappear from the immediate surroundings. At every stage, gardeners have the opportunity to engage in these processes. Passively you anticipate the changes that the various seasons and weather patterns may bring, while actively you make choices that change the current garden into the one that is in your mind.

I regularly visit the Chelsea Flower Show in London, which takes place during the third week of May each spring. The show gardens grab everyone's attention, each brought to perfection for just five brief days of adulation. On returning to my own garden things are usually very different. The glamour of the early spring bulb displays are just a memory, the roses, not having been forced into bloom for a show, are still in bud and apart from the off-white flowers of goat's beard the garden is overwhelmingly green. Where are the drifts of vibrant lupins, the battalions of blue delphinium spires, the perfume of wisteria blossom, and the tunnels dripping with golden laburnum tassels above bobbing allium pompoms? Nowhere, of course, and how easy it is to feel disappointed with one's efforts. However, the reality is that a garden is for every day – and not just six days in the third week of May. Space generally needs to be reserved for plants that perform at other times of the year, and so you must choose what you want, and when, because no garden can be at its peak every day of the year.

Sometimes it will be the plants themselves that encourage you to grow them and develop them into a bold planting theme. On other

occasions, you may choose to bring your beds and borders to a crescendo at a given week or month in the year or maybe to concentrate on one season. Each plant creates an impact at a particular time of the gardening year and, when flowering is its main attraction, its contribution to the garden may be limited to a very short time frame indeed. Its powerful presence may catch your eye because of its colour, habit, or the contrasts that it can make with nearby plants. Outside its seasonal peak it should ideally contribute something

more to the garden scene, such as impressive seed heads, berries, autumn tints, or a bold winter silhouette. It must also be capable of thriving in the local growing conditions.

Here in "Seasonal Themes" perennials are grouped and described in terms of their main seasonal impact. The plants have been drawn from the planting schemes of different gardeners and designers who have chosen to use perennials to create bold designs.

Moving through the year from early stirrings of plants in late winter to the lofty windswept grandeur of autumn, this section analyzes each season for the possibilities it offers in terms of mood and weather, as well as the specific plants that reach their peak at such a time. Not every perennial flowering in each season will be covered, but rather those that when used effectively can make a considerable impact on their surroundings and be developed into eye-catching planting themes. Hopefully the following pages will inspire you to make your own choices from the extensive range of possibilities.

ABOVE The prairie planting scheme in the Hermannshof garden, Weinheim, is dominated by *Penstemon digitalis* and its red-leaved form, *P.d.* 'Husker Red', in early summer.

PREVIOUS PAGES In early summer *Salvia nemorosa* and *Achillea* 'Coronation Gold' can also create a bold planting theme, which remains interesting when the flowers fade and form attractive seed heads.

Winter

LEFT This garden is made entirely from perennials, including bleached ornamental grasses which battle throughout the winter months with the cold, the rain, and, here, the wind. Many different cultivars of *Miscanthus sinensis* and other warm-season grasses flower in late summer. They are capable of retaining their seed heads and shape during winter, to extend the season of interest.

RIGHT Many ferns such as polystichum are evergreen and gain impact in winter, as here when etched with early morning frost.

Although for some people the best season to start writing a book about the excitement of gardening with perennials would be in high summer, when surrounded by rippling displays of daisies, coneflowers, veronica spires, and waving ornamental grasses, for me it was necessary to start in the depths of winter using memories, notes, and photographs as my guides. It would have been convenient to launch into the well-trodden clichés of winter and extol the splendours of grasses and seed heads dusted with early morning frost, however the weather had been wet and windy and many perennials in my garden had begun to topple over. With frost and snow seeming an ever-rarer occurrence for capturing those alluring images so much a feature of gardening magazines in winter, I was in danger of floundering until I decided to visit Beth Chatto's famous perennial garden in Essex.

My boat from Holland to England arrived sufficiently early to enable me to enter Beth Chatto's garden at opening time. Heavy dew encrusted every leaf and sparkled in the bright sunshine. Had the temperature been around freezing perhaps those pictures of frost-fringed foliage would have been possible, but the warmth made it a pleasure to be outside in the still and silent air. The gravel garden there occupies the former visitor car park and its planting scheme is an experiment in which drought-tolerant plants are grown in poor soil – in perhaps the driest part of the British Isles. Many of the plants are shrubby in character; they retain their foliage through winter and therefore give the planting a year-round impact. Perennials play a significant role throughout the year although in winter, surely, less so.

Amid the shrubby salvias, cistus, and lavenders, fine ornamental grasses were still

ABOVE *Bergenia* 'Rosi Klose' thrives in Beth Chatto's gravel garden in Essex, England, where it relishes the well-drained conditions in the old car park.

looking effective. The grasses were *Poa labillardierei, Stipa tenuissima, S. splendens, Ampelodesmos mauritanica*, and *Pennisetum macrourum*. They had all perfectly adapted to the extreme conditions in Beth Chatto's garden, and hence grew sturdily and remained compact. In rich damp soil, the same grasses would have grown tall and lush, and all too quickly have fallen victim to stormy winter weather.

Adding to the evergreen structure of her garden and making an important contribution to it were various members of the euphorbia family. The largest of these, *Euphorbia characias* subsp. *wulfenii*, stands more than 1.2m (4ft) high, forming domes of blue-grey foliage almost as wide as they are tall. In early and mid-spring it carries huge domed flower heads. However, a lower-growing species, *E. seguieriana*, was still in flower in winter, having no doubt begun to throw up its yellow frothy flower heads atop rich red stems, some 80cm (32in) tall, ever since

early summer. One other flower attracts attention at this quiet time of the year. It is *Galanthus reginae-olgae* subsp. *reginae-olgae* Winter-flowering Group, which begins flowering in autumn. With so little competition from other blooms, the drifts of this diminutive bulb made quite a bold feature.

Although Beth Chatto's garden was certainly putting forward a good case for perennials in the winter garden, albeit in the very specific conditions of her situation, it was one plant above all others that stole the show for me. This was a revelation as I had always considered bergenias to be rather boring plants, their coarse foliage being aptly described in their common English name of elephant's ears.

Bergenias are common groundcover perennials with bold evergreen foliage and short spikes of pink or white flowers in spring. Here in the gravel garden they are used as full stops – as Beth Chatto describes them –

in the various island beds that make up the free-form design of this riverbed-inspired planting scheme. Bold clumps sweep around the edges of sections of the planting, tidily containing them. Their repetition throughout the garden reinforces the design.

Among the successful cultivars there are *B.* 'Abendglocken', *B.* 'Admiral', *B.* 'Mrs Crawford', and *B. cordifolia* 'Rosa Schwester', whose foliage develops rich tints of red and mahogany in the colder months, while others such as *B.* 'Bressingham Ruby', *B.* 'Rosi Klose', *B.* 'Morgenröte', and *B.* 'Schneekönigin' are especially effective when in flower.

One reason bergenias work so well in Beth Chatto's garden is the very dry, gravelly soil in which they are growing. In rich damp soils, bergenia foliage becomes blackened and rots during damp winters. Wind and slugs can also take their toll, all too often revealing bare twisted stems and ugly stunted growing tips. Bergenias need good drainage, as might be found on a rock garden or raised bed, yet even when their foliage is decimated in winter they quickly recover in spring and flower reliably.

Having learnt about Beth Chatto's bold use of bergenias you might decide to give them another chance, particularly cultivars with smaller leaves that colour well in winter. *B.* 'Wintermärchen', for example, has twisted leaves that reveal their rich red undersides and *B. purpurascens* 'Irish Crimson' produces rounded, shiny, bronze-red winter foliage.

Another reason the bergenias in Beth Chatto's gravel garden are so effective is that they are planted in very large patches never less than 2m (6½ft) long and often more than 1m (3ft) deep. In smaller gardens, little

clumps of bergenias too easily draw attention to their coarse and often untidy foliage rather than function as contrasting elements within the wider design. One way to overcome this might be to use them in slightly raised planting areas of regular shape, possibly isolated within areas of paving or gravel.

Discovering a new plant and thinking of the best ways of exploiting its qualities within a planting design have been my primary motivation as a gardener. Bergenias are an example of how blinkered gardeners can be at times. All too often it is not the plant that is at fault but the ways it has been used that are off-putting. As this survey of planting themes throughout the seasons unfurls, you will be shown original ways of using familiar plants and hopefully you will be inspired to invent your own solutions. In gardening art there are no fixed rules apart from the discipline of selecting plants that thrive in the available conditions. A badly grown bergenia will never make you want to grow it, but when you see it used well it becomes a source of inspiration and often of excitement.

ABOVE The green of *Festuca mairei* is here tempered by the tans of the other stems and seed heads shrouded in early morning mist.

LEFT *Sedum telephium* 'Matrona' looks marvellous when dusted with frost on a cold winter's day.

Winter Weather

Moods in the winter garden can quickly swing from melancholy and wild to magical as wind, rain, and mists give way to sunshine, frosts, and snow. A well-designed garden stands up to scrutiny primarily on its form and overall structure. Paths, walls, hedges, and trees will be its determining features, with perennials serving to reinforce the design, whether they function as evergreen groundcover or remain effective as winter silhouettes.

Flower colour is hardly a consideration at this time of the year because winter colours are muted, with golds and tans dominating, so you need to adjust your focus and hone in on the subtle details, in order to get the most out of such winter landscapes. To some gardeners, a clump of miscanthus grass buffeted by a winter's gale with its tattered seed heads glistening in filtered sunlight is exhilarating, but to others its dead foliage is simply an untidy intrusion that needs to be tidied away.

The true magic arises with the realization that a large area of miscanthus can become transformed into a raging foaming sea, or alternatively a crystalline fairytale landscape, when the weather conditions allow. As ever, garden makers enter a dialogue with nature, set the stage, and then follow the ensuing processes as they unfurl.

BELOW Such a seasonal spectacle is transient. Within three minutes of capturing this image of *Panicum virgatum* grasses and seed heads the sun had risen and melted this enchanting, frost-etched, fairytale landscape.

Planting Themes

Ground-covering perennials are functional rather than spectacular, serving to furnish the garden throughout the worst days of winter. Ornamental grasses can serve the same role, but may also be developed as a more dramatic theme when used in sufficient quantity and variety. The grass garden illustrated on p.108 is a good example. Different forms of miscanthus dominate this garden. They begin to flower in mid- to late summer, here in combination with a mix of late-flowering perennials. At their peak these borders are overflowing with foliage and flowers, but as winter approaches their bulk begins to thin, dark-tinted silhouettes begin to appear, and the grasses seem to stiffen, readying themselves for the onslaught of the wind, rain, and worse that awaits them.

Such schemes represent the culmination of the gardener's plans. The plants will have steadily grown up throughout spring and summer to reach their ultimate size and to achieve their maximum impact. In this sense, winter represents the end of the gardening year; it is a time to stop and reflect and to

make plans for the coming season. Yet winter is also the start of a new cycle of growth and filled with anticipation.

As much as I enjoy the grasses in winter, I soon begin to long for spring and high summer and any signs that nature is moving in that direction are welcome. When eventually the grasses are cut down and the debris left by last year's perennials is cleared away, the garden feels bare and vulnerable. Yet already the stage is set for the first of the new season's planting themes and the search is on for the first noses of snowdrops.

These bulbs, along with winter aconites and cyclamen, are the cast for the first true garden spectacles of the new growing year. Seizing the blank canvas they are capable

Snowdrops and iris decorate the base of willows in late winter, before the leaf canopy forms.

of flooding it with pools of yellow, drifts of pink, and sheets of sparkling white. In parks and large gardens such bulbous plants can be naturalized in grassland to spectacular effect, while in small gardens these small-flowered plants need to be planted where they can create an appropriate impact.

A large colony of winter aconites, the common form *Eranthis hyemalis*, looks wonderful growing along the base of a hedge. Its narrow green leaves will form a ruff behind the golden-yellow "chalices", which open in the sharp sunshine of a winter's day. Their wide splash of colour so early in the year is always so welcome as it signals that the gardening year is once more back on track.

Cyclamen are tougher than their diminutive stature would imply. *Cyclamen coum* may begin to flower in early winter and can continue to brave the elements through to early spring. Its reflexed petals may be white, pink, or sharply tinted with magenta and crimson. The leaves are dull green but often attractively marked with silver patterns. Cyclamen are tolerant of tree-root competition as long as they receive plenty of moisture during winter and spring, when they are in active growth; and when they are happy, they will spread by seeding themselves around.

Old gardens often boast wide drifts of these sophisticated perennials sweeping around the trunks and knotted roots of ancient trees. In smaller spaces cyclamen work especially well when used as part of a mixed planting, bringing variety to a display of snowdrops.

These bulbous perennials are unquestionably the stars of winter. Everyone, including non-gardeners, eagerly awaits the arrival of snopwdrops like the return of an old friend. They have subtle differences, and the more you look the more these became apparent. Some snowdrops are enormous, in snowdrop terms at least, while others produce double flowers and/or bear different green markings on their petals.

For bold drifts, the best species to plant is common snowdrop (*Galanthus nivalis*) or the slightly more vigorous double snowdrop *G.n.* f. *pleniflorus* 'Flore Pleno'. These can spread rapidly by offset bulbs and seed, and you can speed their progress by dividing their clumps in spring, just after they finish flowering.

Many among the "collector's" snowdrops are selections and hybrids involving other species, in particular *G. elwesii* and *G. plicatus*. These are generally larger than *G. nivalis*, with bolder flowers and thereby capable of making a greater garden impact.

Most of these types are too prized and too expensive to plant in large numbers. However, over time and with regular division many could be used in this way. Among the loveliest unusual snowdrops is *G.* 'S. Arnott', which bears glistening white bells held more than 30cm (1ft) high. It grows vigorously and is becoming readily available.

Within a confined space individual plant details become more significant, and so collections of unusual snowdrops need positioning especially carefully. Various winter-flowering shrubs and trees, both deciduous and evergreen, may be introduced in the background. In my garden, for example, the hedge-backed border has upright clumps of snowdrops contrasted with pools of *Cyclamen coum* scattered among a diminutive, rolling landscape formed by various species of hellebores and *Arum italicum* subsp. *italicum* 'Marmoratum'.

The foliage of bold spiky *Helleborus argutifolius* and *H. lividus* as well as finger-thin *H. foetidus* makes such a year-round contribution to the garden that this is possibly more important than the late winter, cream-green flowers. On the other hand, the innumerable cultivars of *H.* x *hybridus* (syn. *H. orientalis*) are grown primarily for their flowers, yet in the garden you can only appreciate the photogenic qualities of these plants if you scramble around on your hands and knees in order to see their hanging, bell-shaped, beautifully speckled flowers properly. Such hellebores, however, are invaluable in the winter garden, giving some height and plenty of colour over many months.

Arum italicum subsp. *italicum* 'Marmoratum' seems to go against convention, reaching its peak in winter and vanishing in summer. This common garden plant is usually known under the incorrect name of *Arum italicum* 'Pictum'. In late summer all there is to see are green stems, thicker than a pencil and some 30cm (1ft) high, with the top half of the stem bearing pealike berries. The berries quickly change from green to bright red and look good for a couple of months. In autumn the leaves emerge and unroll, to become the shape of large arrow heads. Its spectacular leaves are dark glossy green and their veins are highlighted in creamy silver. The solid mounds of leaves remain beautiful until the following summer, so this is one of the most important background plants for any spring border. Dotted here and there and especially towards the back of the border, *Arum italicum* subsp. *italicum* 'Marmoratum' gives bulk and structure to the loose drifts of bulbs that may eventually grow up to surround them.

Winter aconites (*Eranthis hyemalis*) and common snowdrop (*Galanthus nivalis*) carpet this deciduous woodland in late winter in The Netherlands.

Garden Maintenance

At the end of the growing season deciduous perennials lose their leaves and withdraw their resources to below ground. In those cases when their dead foliage remains upright and attractive it is a useful feature in the garden, but the minute it is toppled by wind, rain, or snow it should be cleared away.

Early winter maintenance is all about removing the chaos in the garden and retaining anything that still looks good. It is surprising what a difference half an hour's tidying-up can make. Because the foliage of *Helleborus* x *hybridus* is prone to fungal disease, it is best cut away at this time, to remove any sources of infection from the new flower shoots and leaves, which start to emerge early in the new growing year. Old epimedium foliage should also be removed by early winter, as if left it can obscure their delicate, early spring flowers. If you leave this task too late, you may cut their promiscuous flower buds, which would be a real pity.

Even though some dead plant material could remain in beds and borders until early spring and meanwhile offer protection to the crowns of plants, a point of compromise needs to be found when they are full not only of summer-flowering perennials but also of early spring-flowering bulbs and perennials. In The Netherlands, late winter is the perfect season for clearing jobs, because the tulips are still underground and so are not damaged by any work at surface level. However, in the case of a snowdrop border, this season would be too late, because some forms come into flower in early winter.

Once they have been scoured, raked, and weeded, perennial beds and borders should end the winter clean and ready to receive their new dose of growth and colour. Timing is everything, and yet the work goes smoothly enough in the cooler temperatures when the dead plant material has lost its bulk and is light and easily cleared away.

FURTHER WINTER-SEASON PERENNIALS

Arum
Height of foliage: 20–40cm (8–16in)
Height in flower: 40cm (16in)
Grows best in moist fertile soil in sheltered, partially shade sites; however, it is remarkably tolerant of dry shade once it has become established.
The bold, arrow-shaped leaves with their distinctive, pale variegated veination of *A.i.* subsp. *italicum* 'Mamoratum' remain in pristine condition throughout winter and make the perfect backdrop for spring bulb displays. The name is frequently confused with *A. italicum* 'Pictum', which is a plain-leaved perennial, attractive but less spectacular and hardy only in sheltered mild situations. The common lords and ladies (*A. maculatum*) has glossy green leaves with irregular dark markings. It is best suited to wilder informal areas of gardens, where the more decorated arum varieties can look out of place.
From time to time other cultivars are offered with more dramatic leaf patterns or leaf shapes: for example, *A.* 'Chamelion', with its wider rounded leaves bearing a mottled green pattern, and *A. italicum* subsp. *italicum* 'White Winter', which is smaller growing and has white mottled variegation. Few of these in my experience are an improvement over *A.i.* subsp. *italicum* 'Mamoratum', which has the perfect combination of scale, form, and garden presence.

Crocus tommasinianus 'Ruby Giant'
Height of foliage: 20–30cm (8–12in)
Height in flower: 15cm (6in)
Tolerates both partial shade and full sun, as well as light or heavy soil; is likely to succeed almost anywhere in the garden.
The flowers of all crocuses appear before the grasslike foliage, very early in spring. *C.t.* 'Ruby Giant' is so easy, cheap, and effective in the garden that it must be the first choice for bold effects. Being sterile, it does not seed around like the true species, which might be an advantage or disadvantage depending on where you grow it. The foliage can look rather untidy later on, so plant crocuses where this will not become a problem.

Eranthis hyemalis

Height of foliage: 5–10cm (2–4in)
Height in flower: 10–12cm (4–6in)
Is ideal for dappled shade in soils rich in leaf mould as found at the edges of deciduous woodland; tolerates acid soils but prefers alkaline conditions.

The clear yellow, cup-shaped flowers bear ruffs of plain green leaves. The European winter aconite (*E. hyemalis*) often has the garden landscape to itself when in flower and can look eye-catching over a long distance for such a low-growing plant; it is the best choice for naturalizing. For something different try *E.h.* (Tubergenii Group) 'Guinea Gold', which has large, deep yellow flowers with deeply divided ruffs boldly tinted bronze at the time of flowering, creating a dramatic contrast. In summer the plants disappear and rest as small tubers below ground. Propagation by division of the tubers or plants is best carried out when flowering has just finished.

Galanthus

Height of foliage: 5–15cm (2–6in)
Height in flower: 10–15cm (4–6in)
Prefers a cool, partially shaded site where bulbs will not dry out from baking summer sunshine; a position adjacent to woodland or beneath border shrubs is ideal. Thrives in heavy, neutral to alkaline soils.

For naturalizing in grass and along the woodland edge the small-growing common snowdrop (*G. nivalis*) is the best choice. It may not be as large and dramatic as the rare forms and other species that exchange hands for high prices, but its character is its strength. It looks very delicate and vulnerable at such a harsh time of the year but in reality it is extremely tough. The same qualities apply to *G. woronowii*, which differs from most others in having bright glossy green leaves that set off its delicate flowers especially well. It grows readily, forming large clumps quickly and making attractive early season groundcover.

Helleborus

Height of foliage: 30–40cm (12–16in)
Height in flower: 30–45cm (12–18in)
Thrives in fertile, loamy, calcarious soils that are enriched annually with leaf mould; are usually easy to please in the garden and will even tolerate gravelly and dry soils when established.

Some species with taller, dramatic, clawlike, spiny edged leaves (such as *H. lividus* and *H. argutifolius*) and those with finer, elongated, dark green leaves (*H. foetidus*) make bold foliage plants as well as producing pale yellow to green flowers in late winter and spring. The many forms of *H.* x *hybridus* are primarily grown for the clumps of colourful flowers they throw up in mid-winter, which remain effective for many weeks on into early spring . These plants are slow to increase and will take a few years to make sizeable clumps that look truly effective within a garden design.

ABOVE RIGHT *Arum italicum* subsp. *italicum* 'Mamoratum'

RIGHT *Crocus tommasinianus* 'Ruby Giant'

BELOW AND BELOW RIGHT *Helleborus* x *hybridus* Blackthorn Nursery hybrids

Spring

Bulbs and not "perennials" are the first group of plants to come into mind when most gardeners think of spring. In reality bulbs are perennials returning to flood gardens with colour each year. They differ from typical perennials because they have developed bulbous root systems that store food and energy to enable them to lie dormant when growing conditions are not to their liking.

Spring-flowering bulbs found in woodland conditions typically grow when sufficient moisture and light are available to them and subsequently rest when the tree canopy closes above them and adjacent plants grow up and occupy any available space in early summer. Other spring-flowering bulbs occur in open, exposed situations, where sufficient moisture is only available to them during winter and spring, whereupon they are subjected to a summer baking as dormant bulbs deep underground, as for example with tulips. In either case these spring-flowering bulbs earn their place in the perennial garden because they offer gardeners the first

moisture in spring, and are baked dry for months in summer. With careful selection, however, cultivars can be found that do appear reliably each year within the perennial garden: for example, botanical tulips derived from the early flowering species *Tulipa kaufmanniana, T. fosteriana,* and *T. greigii.* Additionally, the tough Darwinhybrid Group tulips will become established in most gardens, although the size of their flowers in subsequent years will be considerably smaller than those produced by newly planted bulbs.

Personally I do not restrict myself to such tulips but grow many other types that I accept will need to be replaced each year. Such bulbs I consider an essential part of the perennial garden as they can function in two important ways: they can be used to associate with other plants flowering at the same time, to create schemes that evoke the freshness of spring; and also they can provide continuity of interest before the traditional garden perennials have had time to develop their full summer glory.

Low drifts of blue-flowered pulmonarias, white-flowered *Pachyphragma macrophyllum,* and ground-hugging *Anemone blanda* in shades of blue and white create the setting for a display of exciting tulips that begin with bright orange, multi-flowered *Tulipa praestans* 'Fusilier' followed by white-flowered Triumph *T.* 'Pax', and later Lily-flowered *T.* 'White Triumphator'. For contrast, the dark crimson-flowered Triumph *T.* 'Jan Reus' and later Single Late *T.* 'Queen of Night' are planted together with vibrant pinks such as Triumph *T.* 'Attila', Viridiflora *T.* 'Dolls Minuet', and Single Late *T.* 'Grand Style'.

opportunity for bold displays at a time when most other perennials are only just beginning to come into growth.

I am passionate about tulips and use them to create the first seasonal spectacle in my garden. Unfortunately many of the highly bred cultivars are not perennial as most garden soils are too rich in nutrients and too wet throughout summer for these plants, whose ancestors originated in high mountain passes with rocky, well-drained soils that are frozen solid in winter, receive plenty of

Almost more important, however, is the second way that tulips can be used in your garden. They can assist perennial borders to retain their interest during the period when the plants are growing up prior to flowering later in summer. Prairie-style plantings, for example, are dominated by late-flowering perennials such as rudbeckias, asters, solidagos, and vernonias together with

LEFT The flowers of *Darmera peltata* emerge from bare soil prior to the bold foliage, which will provide its primary contribution to the garden through the rest of its growing season.

BELOW Tulips hand over the baton to alliums in late spring. Although yellow, Single Late *Tulipa* 'Big Smile' is still pristine, Lily-flowered *T.* 'Red Shine' is fading fast, while *Allium hollandicum* has just come into flower.

warm-season grasses such as panicums, pennisetums, and miscanthus. In such a scheme in spring, therefore, there is little to see apart from differing tints of green foliage. By flooding the area with tall red tulips, for example, the vibrant colour contrast can create a sensational point of interest. Follow this on with other dramatic bulbous perennials such as *Camassia leichtlinii* subsp. *leichtlinii* (syn. *C. leichtlinii* 'Alba') or *Allium hollandicum* and the area will remain

attractive until the approach of its main season of floral display.

Daffodils (*Narcissus*) are the other main group of spring bulbs to create sensational seasonal effects. The principles for using any of the innumerable cultivars and species are the same: keep the range of varieties and colours simple, use early, mid-, and late season varieties to prolong the display, and avoid the larger cultivars with a scale that is more appropriate to the exhibition table than the open garden. For example, the early nodding flowers of *N. pseudonarcissus* look appropriate when planted along a woodland path as they fit the informal character of such an area. At the back of a formal herbaceous border try wide drifts of one of the small-cupped daffodils such as *N.* 'Barrett Browning', with its wide open, white-petalled blooms surrounding small, orange-marked trumpets. In such a position they create the chorus to any prima donna tulips in the

foreground, and their dull green foliage is quickly obscured by the burgeoning perennials that quickly grow up shortly after these easy daffodils fade. One particular favourite to bring the daffodil season to an end is *N.* 'Pipit', a Jonquilla type with small, lemon-yellow flowers fading to white at their centres. These fresh-faced flowers bring a sparkling contrast to any dark-foliage plants nearby. They can look particularly good when planted next to voluminous clumps of the freshly emerged, purple-brown foliage of *Ligularia dentata* 'Desdemona'.

Weeks earlier, these same ligularias would have been crumpled, fleshy leaves coloured with a medley of purple and beetroot tones. The explosion of growth that quickly followed typifies mid- to late spring, as one by one favourite perennials end their winter sleep. *Gunnera manicata* is undoubtedly the most impressive, with its unfurling leaves that will eventually tower above your head and serve as shelter when it rains. Frost is their enemy this early in the year, and a nearby fleece blanket

ready to offer night protection when forecasts threaten is a sensible safeguard.

The intensity of colour to be found in the emerging foliage of many perennials can itself be useful in developing early spring planting themes. The rich red shoots of many peonies are a classic combination with mid-season tulips – as is their sumptuous dark foliage – long before they themselves flower and dominate their surroundings. Other perennials offer fresher foliage colour for contrast. Many of the summer-flowering crocosmias produce their narrowly sword-shaped foliage very early in the season and can make a positive contribution to a fresh, yellow-green, spring colour scheme. The newly emerging foliage of *Valeriana phu* 'Aurea' is the main reason to grow it, because later the leaves turn plain green at the same time as the plant throws up insignificant, white, umbel flowers.

Undoubtedly important in this category of perennials with attractive young leaves is the daylily (*Hemerocallis*). The foliage of *H. lilioasphodelus* (syn. *H. flava*), for

example, emerges a bright shade of yellow and quickly expands into bold, arching clumps. As a group, daylilies are important in the summer border, but during spring they can also make a significant contribution. Because the different sorts display varying tones from bright yellow to bright green, they could on their own – or better still in combination with tulips – be developed into a strongly patterned, spring theme.

Two bold perennials attract attention to themselves in spring by throwing up striking flowers prior to the emergence of their foliage; one of these you may well want in the garden, and the other possibly not. *Darmera peltata* and the smaller form, *D.p.* 'Nana', produce long, wiry, waist-high flower stems that end in domed clusters of starry, pink-toned flowers. When growing next to water in the damp soil they relish, the effect is doubled by their graceful reflections. Their rounded leaves soon appear and make a striking feature for the rest of the growing season. Interest continues into autumn when frosts occur, causing their leaves to develop attractive tints before retreating below

ground. *Petasites japonicus* in comparison is an aggressive spreader that overwhelms everything in its way. However, its long flower stems bearing buds at regular intervals along their length create a fine architectural feature. The round scalloped foliage is so impressive that where the setting allows it can be used to brilliant effect as a dominating feature for the whole of the ensuing summer.

Many perennials flower in spring and some, like many bulbs, take advantage of the light and moisture to bring woodland areas alive before summer and shade arrive. Many of these come from North America and China and are to be treasured. Where conditions are suitable, drifts of white-flowered trilliums could become an exotic- or native-planting theme, depending on which continent you garden in, although for most gardeners such effects will have to remain a dream.

Easy perennials that can be relied on to create eye-catching effects in most garden plans include ferns and grasses. These might be perfect to create a tranquil woodland planting interspersed with clumps of more delicate treasures that require more time and attention if they are to succeed.

Drifts of colour might be introduced by using various easy perennials, which are often included in the group of perennials termed groundcover such as pulmonarias. The foliage of pulmonarias is attractive, sometimes splashed and spotted in silver, and their flowers in shades of blue, pink, and white

ABOVE *Camassia cusickii* and *Allium hollandicum* 'Purple Sensation' may not always flower at the same time each year, but when they do the interactions of form and colour are enthralling.

LEFT *Persicaria bistorta* flowering at the same time as blue camassia makes an eye-catching display.

are borne over many weeks. Other indispensable groundcover plants include *Brunnera macrophylla*, with its starry blue flowers in mid- to late spring, and low and spreading *Omphalodes verna*, with its small blue flowers. *Pachyphragma macrophyllum* is perhaps less well known but in many ways the star of the group. It flowers very early in the year, producing loose sprays of pure white flowers, very similar to *Brunnera macrophylla*, in a display that continues for weeks on end. These groundcover perennials can be woven together to create a woodland carpet that might become the setting for hellebores that keep flowering well into spring, bulbs such as daffodils and species tulips, and a host of spring-flowering shrubs and trees.

Euphorbias are essential garden plants and make a contribution over a significant part of the year. Of the early-flowering species *E. polychroma* is good in a sunny spot while *E. amygdaloides* var. *robbiae* is suitable for sun or shade. *Euphorbia polychroma* makes a compact dome covered in bright yellow flower "bracts". The plants are in scale with tulips and daffodils and are their obvious partners in an open sunny situation. For some gardeners *E. polychroma* is too stiff and harshly coloured, and they prefer *E. amygdaloides* var. *robbiae* – a spreading sort for woodland-edge situations. Its dark glossy leaves are evergreen and the yellow flowers are borne in loose heads above the foliage. I have used it in combination with Bowles' golden sedge (*Carex elata* 'Aurea')

and the freshly emerging foliage of the grass *Calamagrostis* x *acutiflora* 'Overdam', which in spring has yellow variegation in its leaves later turning silvery white. Together these plants form a frothy yellow horizon, which I find makes a good setting for *Tulipa* 'Black Parrot' and the white and green flowers of the Viridiflora Group *T.* 'Spring Green'.

Among the many wonderful euphorbias to use around gardens, two are indispensable as in late spring they can take over in the planting scheme just described and continue it on into early summer. They are both suitable for damp soil, but are tolerant of drier conditions as well. The largest is *E. palustris*, which has a more informal character than *E. griffithii*. It makes wide clumps up to 1.5m (5ft) tall and bears the yellow flower heads characteristic of the genus. The size and habit of *E. palustris* suggest that it is best used to fill the background in a planting plan, or in the wilder areas of the garden, because after flowering it grows still further, producing numerous unruly wands of fresh, willow-leaved foliage. In autumn the leaves turn a range of wonderful yellows and oranges. The flower heads of *E. griffithii* by contrast are terracotta-orange. This species is available in a range of cultivars with subtly varied tints, of which *E.g.* 'Dixter' is the richest, while a new one, *E.g.* 'Fern Cottage', seems to offer a more subtle tone of pinkish orange.

Like euphorbias, persicarias are a varied group of perennials that have growth habits as different as groundcovering *P. affinis* and monumental, clump-forming *P. polymorpha*. Related plants such as the feared Japanese knotweed (*Fallopia japonica*, syn. *Polygonum cuspidatum*) are aggressive colonizers, while others such as *Persicaria bistorta* are still quite vigorous but far easier to control. *Persicaria bistorta* is also one of the earliest to flower. In *P.b.* 'Superba' the flowers spikes are the shape as a man's finger, but thicker, and the flowers are a clean tone of violet-pink. They thrive in damp conditions in partial shade, and I have seen them looking particularly good when merged into snowy woodrush (*Luzula nivea*). This low-growing, grassy perennial has fine leaves edged with silver hairs, which provide its silvery/snowy appearance. It produces fluffy, off-white flower heads at the same time as persicaria and looks stunning when mixed with the persicaria's contrasting flower heads. Were you to add to this the tall blue flower spikes of camassia the scene would be complete. It too likes similar damp conditions.

Perhaps the most coherent thematic display I know occurs in the late spring garden at the Fairhaven Woodland and Water Garden. Here primulas seed around and have been encouraged on their way by replanting, to create wide drifts in shades of pink and purple. These are the easily grown candelabras such as *Primula pulverulenta* and *P. japonica*. Along paths that wind between native woodland the primulas drift back to combine with other exotics such as skunk cabbage (*Lysichiton americanus*) and *Petasites japonicus*. The repetition of these dominant elements creates a tranquil atmosphere that is at the same time awe-inspiring due to its considerable scale.

BELOW Candelabra primulas line paths that wind their way among natural watercourses. These provide the perfect conditions for the growth of these primulas in the Fairhaven Woodland and Water Garden, Norfolk, England.

FURTHER SPRING-FLOWERING PERENNIALS

Camassia

Height of foliage: 30–40cm (12–16in)

Height in flower: 70–120cm (28–48in)

In gardens, grows best in full sun and damp soil, and seems to revel in heavy clay.

These North American bulbous plants form clumps of grasslike foliage from which tall, elegant flower spikes rise. They are fantastic for adding contrast of form and colour to planting schemes in late spring and early summer. *C. leichtlinii* subsp. *suksdorfii* Caerulea Group produces violet-blue flowers. The foliage is finer than that of ice-blue-flowered *C. cusickii* and the flowering period longer, making this the best choice for thematic schemes. *C. leichtlinii* subsp. *leichtlinii* (syn. *C.l.* 'Alba') is taller, at 1.2m (4ft), and conveniently later flowering than other camassias, while *C. quamash*, growing to only 30–60cm (1–2ft) in flower, is probably at its most useful when naturalized in short grass at the water's edge.

Darmera peltata

Height of foliage: 90cm (36in)

Height in flower: 100cm (39in)

Grows next to water in moist to well-drained soil in sun or partial shade.

Small pink flowers are gathered at the ends of dark hairy stems and appear before the foliage in early spring. The leaves develop from the shallow rhizomes and are held horizontally atop upright leafstalks. They are rounded, up to 40cm (16in) in diameter, are soft green in summer, and later develops attractive autumn tints as temperatures begin to fall. These easy perennials make spectacular groundcover or specimen plants when growing next to water.

Euphorbia

Height of foliage: 30–90cm (12–36in)

Height in flower: 55–120cm (22–48in)

There are species of euphorbia for all seasons and many different garden habitats. In spring the spotlight falls on two euphorbias that thrive in well-drained to moist garden soil in sun or partial shade.

E. amygdaloides var. *robbiae* is a form of wood spurge that spreads by underground runners and may become invasive – unlike the true species. It tolerates dry shade, but grows best in fertile, moisture-retentive soil, where it can become invasive. *E.a.* var. *robbiae* is ideal groundcover in woodland-edge situations as its dark glossy foliage is evergreen. The flower heads remain effective throughout spring, but should be cut away in early summer to make room for new shoots that will flower the following year. In contrast, *E. palustris* is a vigorous, deciduous species that makes huge mounds of fine-leaved foliage. It originates in marshy situations and needs adequate soil moisture to thrive. Its unruly habit and preference for damp soils mean that it is best for naturalizing along the banks of streams and rivers, and in other wild places in gardens.

Iris

Height of foliage: 20–50cm (8–20in)

Height in flower 25–90cm (10–36in)

Grows in soils as different as dry and sun baked to moist and even in shallow water at the margins of lakes and stream. All irises require full sun to flower well. In general, shorter irises flower earlier than taller-growing species and cultivars, and they cover a season from mid-spring to early summer. The bearded irises, which need open, sunny, well-drained situations, are popular for their many hued flowers and their stiff upright foliage. *I.* 'Langport Pagan' is of medium height (35cm/14in) and flowers in late spring. *I. sibirica* is equally important in the perennial border, where it finds the soil and moisture levels that it prefers. Its deciduous foliage emerges very early in spring, making an important design feature in its own right. The flowers – mainly in shades of blue, purple, and white – are bold and effective over many weeks from late spring and the arching foliage remains an attractive feature in the border throughout summer.

BELOW LEFT *Camassia leichtlinii* subsp. *suksdorfii* Caerulea Group.

BELOW *Iris* 'Langport Pagan' in front of *Geranium macrorrhizum.*

Omphalodes

Height of foliage: 10cm (4in)
Height in flower: 15–25cm (6–10in)
Flourishes in shade in humus-rich soil.
Omphalodes generally makes good groundcover. Its
flowers are usually blue, although there are also white-
and violet-coloured cultivars. On *O. cappadocica* clouds
of starry, blue, single flowers hover for weeks in mid-
and late spring above low, spreading clumps of light
green foliage. *O.c.* 'Starry Eyes' is true to its name and
has azure-blue petals neatly edged with white. *O. verna*
is more effective groundcover, making wide, spreading
mats of tidy green foliage. Its blue flowers are smaller
than those of *O. cappadocica*, but nevertheless
effective en masse.

Pachyphragma macrophyllum

Height of foliage: 20cm (8in)
Height in flower: 35cm (14in)
Is easy to grow and will even tolerate dry shade once
established.
White, forget-me-not-like flowers open along with
pulmonarias and early daffodils in early spring and
continue to be effective for many weeks, making
P. macrophyllum an extremely important perennial
for planting schemes in woodland-edge situations. It
throws up clumps of rounded, dark green, glossy leaves,
which make a valuable contribution as groundcover for
the remainder of the growing season. It is surprising
how few gardeners know about this indispensable plant.

Persicaria bistorta 'Superba'

Height of foliage: 30–40cm (12–16in)
Height in flower: 70–90cm (28–36in)
Originates in damp meadows in northern Eurasia; in
gardens it grows best in moist and heavy soils in full
sun or partial shade.
The genus *Persicaria* contains some indispensable
border treasures as well as some terrible weeds, and
P. bistorta 'Superba' falls into both categories. In well-
drained borders it is generally easy to control, but in
damp fertile soils it spreads aggressively. It bears wide,
lilac-pink flower spikes, which are thicker and more
formal than the species.

Primula

Height of foliage: 25cm (10in)
Height in flower: 50–70cm (20–28in)
Requires rich, moisture-retentive soil in situations
that provide shelter from drying winds; given sufficient
moisture, grows happily in full sun or partial shade.
In mid-spring *P. denticulata* produces flower clusters
at the end of stems, and they resemble drumsticks.
In woodland settings they can make drifts in shades
of pink, purple, and white. At only 30cm (1ft) tall,

P. denticulata lacks the drama offered by the
candelabra primulas, which flower slightly later. With
flowers arranged in whorls up the stems, *P. japonica*
is the first primula in spring to bear its rich crimson
or pink flowers. *P. pulverulenta* blooms at the end of
spring on into early summer, with elegant flower stems
covered in a white mealy patina. The flowers are intense
crimson-purple or pale in some selections such as the
well-known *P.p.* Bartley hybrids.

Pulmonaria

Height of foliage: 20–30cm (8–12in)
Height in flower: 30–50cm (12–20in)
Grows in shade or partial shade but needs humus-rich
soil that remains moist throughout the growing season;
tolerates drought but then becomes disfigured by mildew.
P. 'Blue Ensign' has dark green, plain leaves with a
rumpled sculptural quality. The pure deep blue flowers
are the largest of any pulmonaria, making this the best
within this colour range. There are also pink- and white-
flowered forms, most with bold leaves splashed and
spotted with silver. Some pulmonarias are grown for
their exceptional, silver-marked foliage. For example,
P. 'Opal' makes dense clumps of heavily silver-marked
leaves, and in spring bears generous quantities of pale
blue flowers. *P. rubra* 'Redstart' with its coral red
flowers and coarse, pale plain green foliage forms
useful groundcover, while *P.r.* 'David Ward' has a wide
white margin to its pale green leaves, but these scorch
easily so the plant needs to be sited in light shade.

Omphalodes cappadocica
'Starry Eyes' with ostrich
fern (*Matteuccia
struthiopteris*).

Pulmonaria **'Blue Ensign'**

Early Summer

LEFT *Hemerocallis* 'Little Bugger', upright *Stachys officinalis* 'Hummelo', the grass *Imperata cylindrical* 'Rubra', and the annual colour of snapdragons (*Antirrhinum*) combine to display summer's excess next to a garden pond.

BELOW *Aruncus dioicus* makes a dramatic spectacle in this woodland setting in early summer.

The search is on for summer planting themes the moment tulips end in late spring. After so much excitement and colour, a change to pace and calm is sometimes called for. It will not be long before roses begin to flower in abundance, and these together with blue-flowered catmints – *Nepeta* 'Six Hills Giant' or better still the taller-growing *N. racemosa* 'Walker's Low' – mark summer's true beginning. However, there may be a slight pause between these two seasonal highlights.

At this transitional stage, many gardens are mostly green, which is a beautiful and restful colour and can take many forms. Ferns, hostas, and other bold foliage plants such as rodgersias, darmeras, and ligularias will all be looking fresh and full. Late-season perennials and grasses will be growing vigorously, and hedges such as beech and hornbeam never look better than at this early

time. In many perennial gardens *Euphorbia palustris* will still be filling the background with its fresh chartreuse-tinted flower heads, yet the stars of the moment are frequently aruncus. Although it is native to moist woodland, aruncus can tolerate drought and is therefore suitable for a wide range of growing conditions in gardens and parks.

Goat's beard (*A. dioicus*) is to be found in many gardens, usually putting on a good show in dry shade somewhere in the background. As its Latin name suggests, plants are of either one sex or the other. The males have fluffier and more dramatic flower heads, but these are very short-lived, perhaps a week if you are lucky. The female flower heads are more elegant and open and have the bonus of seed capsules that extend their season of interest. However, they can release lots of seed. Unless you get a section from a clump

Lupins flowering in early summer are accent plants amid the mass of *Anthemis tinctoria* flowers.

tall and maybe somewhat wider. Its foliage is elegantly divided, glossy, and yellow-green. The creamy flower heads fade to buff-brown and remain an attractive feature of the plant for months. *Aruncus aethusifolius* can make unusual and effective groundcover in woodland settings.

The famous German nurseryman Ernst Pagels has recently developed hybrids using *A. aethusifolius* to form a new group of large aruncus with distinctive foliage and heavy flower spikes. Unquestionably the best, *A.* 'Horatio', is the biggest – at around 1m (3ft) tall – with an open, shrublike habit. Its white flowers are gathered into short spikes, which are held at right angles to the dark-coloured flower stems. Like all other aruncus, these flowers quickly turn to brown as they fade, but in this case the colour change progresses along the flower spikes, giving them an attractive, two-tone appearance and thereby extending their season of interest.

Two more of Ernst Pagels' introductions are only half the size of *A.* 'Horatio' and they have finer leaves, which are more similar to those of *A. aethusifolius*. The bright green-leaved *A.* 'Sommeranfang' grows 50cm (1½ft) tall and has a stiff and distinctive flower pattern. In contrast, *A.* 'Woldemar Meier' has a noticeably overhanging habit and is probably the more elegant of the two.

The different forms of aruncus look best when standing alone as specimens in the garden; this suits their character best. By placing different forms throughout the garden you can achieve both the emphasis that repetition brings to garden design, albeit with subtle variations, and differentiations that add an extra layer of complexity to your planting compositions.

Also flowering in these early days of summer is a favourite perennial, *Persicaria polymorpha*. Unlike some persicarias, or polygonums as they were once called, the rootstock of *P. polymorpha* is so compact that propagation by division is difficult and the best method is to take summer stem cuttings,

of known gender, you are unlikely to know which sex of plant you have until it flowers.

The shrublike clumps of elegant foliage of *A. dioicus* are attractive all summer. Although its floral season is short, the subtle changes it exhibits as it edges towards flowering are its most endearing feature. Hundreds of tiny green buds become steadily paler until they whiten to resemble grains of rice before opening to create the showy flower plumes.

Aruncus dioicus 'Glasnevin' is a good cultivar for screening purposes during summer. Fine, open flower heads produce very white flowers before quickly fading. This is an old cultivar, as is *A.d.* 'Kneiffii', which has finely divided leaves that look as if they have been attacked by an army of caterpillars. It is a smaller plant than the others and so ideal for small gardens. Taller growing and slightly later flowering than these is *A.d.* 'Zweiweitenkind', which is in a class of its own. There is a warm brown tinge to its leaves, and its clear white flowers are finer and held with delicate poise above the foliage.

The much smaller-growing *A. aethusifolius* is a good garden plant, reaching 30cm (1ft)

which root very easily. This plant luxuriates in heavy clay soil, and can grow more than 2m (6½ft) tall. From its compact base the sturdy stems spread out to occupy a space nearly as wide as it is high, but without needing any staking. Only when it starts to elbow its neighbours sideways may intervention be necessary and that will have been the fault of the gardener for placing them too closely together in the first place and not the plant itself, which is an amiable border perennial.

The soft white flowers of *P. polymorpha* are small and massed together in loose heads at the ends of its numerous stems. They are continuously produced for at least two months, fading to cream and then flushed pink before eventually melting away out of consciousness. With its coarse, soft green leaves, it creates a dominant but subtle billowing feature in the background and fits perfectly into a calm green planting theme.

Brighter colours are eager to re-enter the stage during summer. Biennial foxgloves are keen to seduce but if chosen primarily for their slim upright form it is best to plant the the more restrained, white and apricot-tinted cultivars. Aquilegias are also irrepressible, appearing spontaneously to introduce the cottage-garden mood to a garden. Like lupins, you may prefer to use them as biennials, as after flowering their contribution is minimal. The aquilegias return without help, and the lupins can be grown from seed elsewhere and returned to the borders in late summer.

Lupins with their vibrant colours and bold upright flower spikes are good for a strong planting theme. They can be removed from borders once their flowering is finished, to release space for later-flowering perennials growing nearby. If left in situ they invariably become affected by mildew later in the summer, creating an eyesore for far too long.

Aruncus dioicus 'Zweiweltenkind' with *Persicaria polymorpha* signal the start of summer in my garden.

The purple flower heads of tall-growing ornamental onions are a far easier way of bringing a wash of colour to your perennial borders this early in the summer. *Allium hollandicum* and its darker-flowered *A.h.* 'Purple Sensation' are deservedly popular. It is so easy to slip their bulbs in between the perennials and, unlike many tulips, they are far more likely to return year on year. Ornamental onions work especially well as their foliage appears early and nourishes their bulbs before they flower. When in bloom, their ball-shaped flower heads are held clear of their neighbour's rapidly growing foliage. If tall and vigorous perennials swamp these 1m (3ft) high ornamental onions half way through their display, replace them with the much taller, white-flowered *Allium* 'Mount Everest' or light purple *A. giganteum*, both with slightly smaller flower heads. The opposite extreme is offered by *A.* 'Globemaster', with flower heads easily 20cm (8in) across and

filled with a mass of rich violet flowers. Its dramatic flowers remain colourful and are effective far longer than the others, and although its bulbs are expensive you need far fewer to create a really impressive display.

There are many more excellent ornamental onions to use in the gardens, but two that are indispensable along the front of borders are *A. cristophii* and *A. schubertii*. Both stay below knee height and bear open flower heads that resemble shooting-star firework displays. They look stunning floating amid frothy grasses such as *Agrostis nebulosa*, *Festuca amethystina*, and *Stipa tenuissima*.

So far everything that has been described is either calm or sophisticated, but these are not words that can be applied to oriental poppies – even when their colours are soft and seductive. *Papaver orientale* is capable of being the flamboyant star in your early summer garden. Its huge flowers are in a sumptuous range of colours, from white

BELOW Both *Valeriana pyrenaica* and *Allium hollandicum* bring early summer colour to perennial borders.

and soft pale pink to vibrant oranges and glowing reds. The appeal lies in their bombastic character tempered by a short flowering period. Were they to flower all summer gardeners would quickly tire of them, but for two weeks in early summer they can strike just the right note of excess. After flowering their foliage rapidly becomes unsightly and is best removed. Provided they are fed and watered, oriental poppies will replenish their foliage, but they generally wait until autumn to make their reappearance.

Hardy geraniums are an essential component of the summer garden. Some such as *Geranium macrorrhizum* and *G. endressii* are common ground-covering perennials, while others such as hard pink *G.* x *riversleaianum* 'Russell Prichard' and blue *G. sylvaticum* 'Amy Doncaster' extend their flower stems far and wide, weaving their way among neighbouring plants.

When it comes to eye-catching effects, some of the larger-growing cultivars of hardy geranium are the most important. In warm-temperate climates *G. maderense* makes bold mounds, up to 1m (3ft) across, smothered in bright magenta flowers, but it is not reliably hardy. Not so floriferous but still outstanding is *G. psilostemon*, but each plant does take up a lot of room and can easily smother its neighbours. Its flowers are a dark shade of magenta with a rich black eye. Over the years, various hybrids of this large geranium have been released. For example, *G.* 'Patricia' is like its parent but flowers for longer and again in autumn – the flowers coming in a slightly lighter shade of pink. It goes well with greenish white aruncus and soft lilac-pink persicaria to inject a sprinkling of sharp colour contrast. *Geranium* 'Ann Folkard' is a yellow-leaved hybrid, and there are many more. What is important about these bold geraniums is that their strong colour impact can work in a garden's design to link its various parts together. By planting clumps of *G. psilostemon* cultivars in several borders within the garden, they gain unity.

Some hardy geraniums are cultivated primarily for their foliage – their flowers coming as a bonus. *Geranium phaeum* var. *phaeum* 'Samobor' has large, mid-green leaves with a bold, black-brown band across the middle. It grows to 40cm (16in) and is best planted in semi-shade, where its sombre colouring can bring dramatic contrasts beside yellow- or golden-leaved plants. The leaves of *G. phaeum* 'Variegatum' have irregular white edges and ruby-red streaks. *Geranium phaeum* 'Margaret Wilson' is more refined, with regular bands of green and yellow-white. Its flowers are also a plus point, being a shade of purple that harmonizes perfectly with its foliage.

TOP Throughout summer the flower and then seed heads of ornamental onions contribute to the perennial border, as here, where heads of *Allium cristophii* hover amid purple-flowered *Origanum* 'Rosenkuppel'.

ABOVE A vigorous clump of *Geranium* 'Patricia' brings a strong shot of colour to this otherwise tranquil, early summer scene.

Geranium renardii is instantly recognized by the felted texture on its grey-green, chunky foliage. When planted at the front of a bed or border, it makes a perfect foil for any bright-flowered neighbour.

Astrantias became a very fashionable summer theme a few years ago, after Piet Oudolf and Arne Maynard's show garden had won "Best in Show" at the Chelsea Flower Show. In it, a glorious, Persian-carpet effect had been created using dark red-flowered *Astrantia major* cultivars such as *A.m.* 'Claret' and *A.m.* 'Ruby Wedding', combined with the purple-flowered thistle *Cirsium rivulare* 'Atropurpureum'. If you find these dark astrantias gloomy, you may prefer the pale forms such as *A. major* subsp. *involucrata* 'Canneman', *A.m.* subsp. *involucrata* 'Shaggy', and pink *A.m.* 'Roma'.

Another popular plant is alstroemeria, even though it is not always successful in

the perennial garden. These plants throw up masses of beautiful flowers in the most desirable colours, tints, and patterns, yet every clump has to be well supported if it is not to collapse untidily. For colour combinations, alstroemerias are exceptional but what other aspect of these plants is of use in the perennial garden? In my search for plants with character that make a useful contribution to a garden at their peak of flowering as well as at other times in the growing season, the colour alone offered by alstomerias is surely not enough.

Magazine articles extol the virtues of the ever-so-trendy penstemons, and they certainly bring considerable colour to the garden throughout the summer. The large-flowered penstemons bear tubular flowers like foxgloves, but in a range of vivid colours, some two toned. I have long been of the opinion that they have very little grace and

Astrantia major 'Ruby Wedding' with *A.m.* 'Roma' behind are two popular, well-coloured plants that thrive in not-too-dry, fertile soil in sun or partial shade.

character and that the flowers are too large. The fact that they are not always hardy means that they require too much extra work to deserve a place in my garden.

A visit to the Hermannshof garden in Weinheim, Germany, early in the summer, however, was a revelation as it demonstrated to me the potential of the small-flowered penstemons and in particular *Penstemon digitalis* and its dark-leaved form *P.d.* 'Husker Red' (*see p.74*). Growing erect to almost 1m (3ft), the light-coloured, tubular flowers were effective over a long distance. The plants had been allowed to seed around and were planted in wide drifts throughout the whole garden. Not only does *P. digitalis* flower for a very long time but the seed heads are also attractive and the plants develop rich russet tints in autumn. In other words, here is a plant that is really earning its keep, and it is also worth noting that it is one of the hardiest species of penstemon. I could imagine Heiner Luz using this plant as one of the leading-aspect perennials in his mixtures for public spaces, because in the Hermannshof garden it was effectively bringing early season interest to a large area of prairie plantings, most of which would not begin flowering until much later in summer.

Delphiniums are another essential perennial garden plant, although they can prove difficult to use as the basis of a thematic planting scheme. Once again it is their character that is at fault. They are generally grown for their splendid columns of flowers, which contrast strongly with rounded shapes nearby. Unfortunately, out of flower, they contribute nothing and are best cut down early in the hope of stimulating a second show of flowers in early autumn.

When looking at many other summer-flowering perennials this same shortcoming is often relevant. Such plants work best as part of a mixed border in which they accent combinations and bring elements of colour or texture to the scene, rather than being given the leading role in their own right.

A BOLD SCHEME FOR MID-SUMMER

A particularly effective scheme for early to mid-summer is also to be found at the Hermannshof garden, in Weinheim. There, the flower spikes of salvias, which bring rich colour, usually blue, and a distinctive shape, occur at the same time as achilleas with their characteristic, flat-topped flower heads, which when yellow can resemble pancakes floating across the border (*see pp.104–5 and 137*). By mixing the two totally contrasting shapes and colours of achilleas and salvias, an eye-catching planting design has been created.

Salvia nemorosa, its cultivars, and various hybrids made with *S. pratensis* are among the most frequently encountered perennials in contemporary planting schemes. *Salvia nemorosa* 'Ostfriesland' was one of the first plants introduced by Ernst Pagels shortly after setting up his nursery in West Germany more than 60 years ago. To this day it remains one of the most useful perennials, and is especially popular with garden designers, who plant this 40cm (16in) high cultivar en masse to create wide sheets of violet-blue colour in early summer. Ernst Pagels followed this salvia with many others, including *S.* x *sylvestris* 'Mainacht', which is taller and earlier flowering in a deeper shade of violet-blue, *S.* x *s.* 'Blauhügel', which is light blue, and the white form *S.* x *s.* 'Schneehügel'.

Interesting effects can be created with these and other salvias when different forms in darker and lighter shades of blue, violet,

The upright spikes of delphiniums are indispensable in early summer. Here they rise above rounded clumps of *Lysimachia ciliata*.

BELOW RIGHT The erect flower stems of *Phlomis tuberosa* 'Amazone' remain a feature from summer through to winter.

BELOW After flowering, the well-textured *Salvia nemorosa* seed heads continue to introduce vertical patterns to planting schemes; they are seen here in mid-summer.

amethyst, and pink are mixed together to create a tapestry of harmonious tints.

It is possible to get a second show of flowers from these salvias, by removing the first flush of flower spikes immediately after their peak. However, many gardeners think it better to leave them and enjoy the medley of green and purple tints that wash over their seed heads all summer as well as the shape of their upright flower pattern, which is such a significant part of their character.

There are taller-growing salvia cultivars to add yet more variation to such early summer schemes. For example, you could try *S.* x *superba* 'Dear Anja' and *S. pratensis* Haematodes Group, with its violet-blue flowers up to 1m (3ft) tall. Both need sun and well-drained conditions to thrive – especially the latter, which in most gardens is considered a short-lived perennial.

Persistence is an important characterisitic that should be sought in any perennials that you add to your garden. However, plants do need the correct growing conditions to thrive, and these are not always what you can offer them. Whether you continue to grow some plants or not is a matter of choice, and in this respect achilleas throw up a challenge. Again, Ernst Pagels and many other nurserymen who have followed his example have introduced a fantastic assortment of medium-height achilleas in a range of sumptuous tints and tones, but they seem to persist for only a year or two. Nevertheless, their horizontal flower heads and colours make them indispensable in many compositions. For public situations and low-maintenance schemes only the toughest forms of these plants should be considered. The tall-growing *Achillea filipendulina* 'Parker's Variety', for example, can thrive in inhospitable clay soil for many years. This is the most typical of achilleas with its large, golden-yellow "plates" of flowers held 1.2m (4ft) high. At the Hermannshof garden, where the emphasis is on low-maintainance public planting, they use the similar cultivar *A.f.* 'Gold Plate' and the lower, brighter yellow *A.* 'Coronation Gold', from which you can

conclude that these are equally persistent forms. Ernst Pagels' *A.* 'Credo' was the first of his attempts to offer a tall-growing achillea in a softer, more easily assimilated, yellow tint. It remains one of the best cultivars but it cannot be called persistent.

Other desirable achillea cultivars are derived from *A. millifolium*. These are lower growing and make spreading clumps. *Achillea* 'Fanal' is a blend of carmine-red and yellow, which mellows as the flower heads age. *Achillea millefolium* 'Paprika' is similar in scarlet and yellow, while *A.* 'Summerwine' bears rich ruby flower heads and is the most persistent in my experience. To summarize therefore: achilleas are quite unusual, offering a strong architectural form that cannot be equalled by any other perennials, and if you want to use them you must accept their weaknesses.

The Hermannshof garden scheme uses many other plants to reinforce the crisscross effect of salvias and achilleas with soft rounded forms of the pale green grass *Festuca mairei* and frothy mounds of *Knautia macedonica* peppered with their scabious-like, rich red flowers emphasizing the horizontal. The verticals are repeated most noticeably by the yellow candelabra flower stems of hybrid verbascums, which are of course biennial and not true perennials. Equally tall *Phlomis tuberosa* 'Amazone' is more subtle, with whorls of flowers arranged at regular intervals up its slim flower stems, which will remain as effective silhouettes throughout winter. The same pattern is also found in the flower stems of *Phlomis russeliana*, but here the clusters of flowers are denser on lower-growing plants. *Veronica longifolia* flower spikes continue the colour theme introduced by the blue salvias on into mid-summer, while another biennial, *Salvia sclarea* var. *turkestanica*, introduces a softer tone with its more robust, mauve flower spikes. For sunny situations this scheme exploits some of the most effective perennials for early summer.

BELOW The achillea and salvia border at the Hermannshof garden, Weinheim, is exemplary.

BOTTOM *Achillea* 'Walther Funcke' and *Eryngium* x *tripartitum* have contasting shapes and textures.

At the height of summer, colour is everywhere in this English mixed border, in which blue campanula, red monarda, yellow daylilies, purple phlox, upright veronica, and frothy geraniums create a visual feast that simply shouts for attention from passers-by.

SUMMER'S EXCESS

As summer progresses more and more perennials come into flower, but many of these are more chorus members than leading role players. Naturally, if you plant enough of any one plant you can develop an effective theme, but a border of only daylilies (*Hemerocallis*) or red hot pokers (*Kniphofia*), for example, will hold little interest once past its peak. One group of plants that might be used to build an effective scheme and also offer opportunities for combinations with many other summer-flowering perennials are the tall, upright-growing veronicas and cultivars of veronicastrum. These sun-loving perennials for well-drained soils have elegant erect flower spikes that call for appropriate counterparts, be these other upright forms or contrasting horizontal ones.

Veronicas come in all shapes and sizes from low-growing and prostrate species to tall elegant border plants. Many flower early in the year and are at home in the conditions offered by the rock garden. For the perennial garden, it is the taller-growing and summer-flowering herbaceous species which are of interest. Their long slim flower spikes are invaluable for introducing upright accents to planting schemes. Additionally, these taller-growing veronicas have their leaves arranged into whorls at regular intervals along their upright stems. This stepped effect contributes to their impact, giving them a presence that far outweighs their actual bulk.

From a gardener's point of view, species of veronica and veronicastrum are viewed as one group. *Veronicastrum virginicum* has contributed some very important, upright plants for the back row of borders. The best of these is undoubtedly *V. virginicum* 'Lavendelturm'. Lavender-blue flowers are borne on long stiff spikes to a height of 1.5m (5ft) from mid-summer until early autumn. Another equally impressive plant is *V.v.* 'Fascination', which has branched flower heads with some of the spikes becoming bent and twisted through a mutation called fasciation. It is similar in colour to *V.v.* 'Lavendelturm', and it too takes a couple of years to reach its full potential in a newly planted scheme. Thereafter *V.v.* 'Fascination' performs without fail year in year out.

Colour in both genera centres around violet-blue, but there are numerous variations as well as white, pink, and red selections. *Veronica longifolia* 'Blauriesin' is the classic rich blue veronica some 60cm (2ft) tall. More subtle is the ice-blue *V.l.* 'Lila Karina'.

A plant that is thought to be a hybrid between veronica and veronicastrum and called *Veronica* 'Inspiration' is of intermediate height at around 1m (3ft). Its pure white flower spikes are characterized by having a slight thickening towards the middle, where the first flowers begin to open. Other taller white forms are *Veronicastrum virginicum* 'Spring Dew', about 1.3m (4¼ft) tall, and *V.v.* 'Diane', which sometimes produces branched flower spikes up to 1.4m (4½ft) tall. The pink tint to be found in *V.v.* 'Alboroseum' is so subtle that the plant is easily mistaken for *V.v.* 'Diane', while the pale pink tint of *V.v.* f. *roseum* 'Pink Glow' is far more effective. Darker still, *Veronica* 'Pink Damask'

Mounds of phlox and vertical spikes of salvias and veronicas are the hallmarks of high summer.

ABOVE *Veronicastrum virginicum* f. *roseum* 'Pink Glow' displays the classic flower spikes of this important group of summer-flowering perennials.

BELOW Those perennials that flower in early summer and form attractive seed heads, such as *Nepeta subsessilis*, should be left undisturbed, to continue their contribution to the border over the months to come.

BELOW RIGHT Summer-flowering *Sedum telephium* 'Matrona' will remain effective throughout summer, autumn, and winter and should therefore be planted near the front of perennial borders.

is an irresistible selection for the front of the border as it reaches only 50cm (1½ft)tall. A recent introduction, *V.* 'Anna', has even darker pink flowers. The last two cultivars can suffer from mildew in late summer and are unfortunately less reliable – that is, more likely to die out – than the rest of the group.

A scheme based on some of these veronicas could be reinforced by other summer-flowering perennials with a similar vertical profile. *Lythrum salicaria* grows wild in damp places and is regularly seen at the water's edge. It is tolerant of drier conditions in garden borders, and its purple-pink flower spikes make an excellent colour contrast with the veronicas. *Lythrum salicaria* 'Zigeunerblut' is a deeper tone than the species, and *L.s.* 'Blush' is light pink. A different character is exhibited by *L. virgatum*, with its finer, branched flower spikes capable of creating a cloudlike mass of intense purple red in the middle of a border.

One of the most widely planted verbenas is *V. bonariensis*, with its clusters of vivid purple flowers held high on fine wiry stems all summer long. In the case of *V. hastata* the flowers are arranged into small spikes in branched flower heads that reach 1.2m (4ft) tall. It seeds around and can overwhelm a border in a couple of seasons. Fortunately, the seedlings are distinctive so readily identified and easy to remove, giving the gardener the opportunity to indulge in a practice that I call creative weeding.

Astilbes are really plants for the waterside and should be used there to create frothy drifts of colour in the dappled shade of summer. They are not appropriate companions for veronicas, although *Astilbe chinensis* var. *taquetii* 'Purpurlanze' is tolerant of drier border conditions and can introduce another variation on the vertical theme with its fluffy candyfloss flower heads.

Grasses are the other obvious verticals to add to a veronica theme, and together they create a tall meadow effect that is the hallmark of naturalistic planting schemes. *Calamagrostis* x *acutiflora* is ideal: having flowered in early summer, it then stands erect with its tan seed heads fully developed. Molinias will be at their peak offering a selection of cultivars that range in height from knee high to well over head height. Meanwhile, miscanthus will be growing vigorously skywards, and will flower later.

Contrast is needed for all these feathery uprights. Flat-topped achillea flower heads could again provide it or the more delicate heads of members of the Apiaceae family with their umbrella shapes. Light and airy fennel and robust angelica are two suitable herbs from this family, as is *Angelica gigas* with its dark maroon, domed flower heads for added impact. Common valerian with a similar habit might also be included to enhance an overtly naturalistic scheme.

Other summer-flowering perennials bring contrast when they grow as rounded masses.

Phlox is the perfect example of this, and its peak is in high summer. Monardas build up into similar bulky mounds in the border at this time, while campanulas can play the same role earlier in the summer and asters later in the year. These are all good perennials capable of being developed into a dominant theme in their own right.

Thalictrums are the very opposite of the verticals, horizontals, and bulky massed plants so for considered. Some favourites rise high into the air, producing diffuse clouds of pretty flowers that float like mist above their border companions. Some like *Thalictrum delavayi* 'Hewitt's Double' are short-lived, but others including *T. rochebruneanum* with its violet-purple flowers and *T. pubescens* (syn. *T. polygamum*) with its creamy white flowers last well. Plants such as these occupy little space in a border, but when in flower can create an extensive effect as they spread their flowers widely in the air above the foliage.

Sedum telephium 'Matrona' is the perfect plant to fill in the front row of a border scheme. In the past gardeners would have used *S.* 'Herbstfreude', with its fleshy green leaves that are effective the moment they appear in spring and are covered with clusters of pink flowers in summer. Its problem has always been that mature clumps fall open and look untidy, but this does not occur with *S. telephium* 'Matrona', which makes similar rounded clumps but the leaves are larger and fleshier in a mixture of tints including pewter and maroon. The light pink flowers appear in summer and being typically arranged into

dome-shaped heads they persist to make effective winter silhouettes.

Already many early summer-flowering perennials such as salvias, achilleas, and nepetas will be producing seed heads that can be left to provide interest in the autumn and winter garden. Veronicas likewise turn shades of tan and brown, to add vertical patterns to your later season pictures. Monardas, which fill the garden with colour in summer, assume a new role in autumn, when the flower heads become dark blobs that outline their once-massive profiles. All these plants should be given equal attention.

RIGHT Naturalistic planting at its peak of emotional expression in summer has been created by Piet Oudolf at Scampston Hall. The planting emphasizes the dynamic processes of nature as well as the transience of superficial beauty. The fading flowers of catmint (*Nepeta*), the knobbly seed heads of *Trifolium rubens*, and the golden clouds of deschampsia grass set the permanent stage for the temporary players, which include the heavy floral mounds of *Monarda* 'Aquarius' and *M.* 'Scorpion', the fragile flowers of *Echinacea pallida*, and the pink spikes of *Teucrium hircanicum*.

High Summer

LEFT *Rudbeckia fulgida* var. *deamii* drifts between the newly emerging flower heads of *Miscanthus sinensis* in my garden, in late summer.

BELOW The frothy, mellow yellow flower heads of *Solidago* 'Goldenmosa' create a colour-coordinated background for *Echinacea purpurea* 'White Lustre'.

The character of the summer garden changes from the calm freshness of its earliest days into the colourful peak at the hottest time of the year and on into the special period that proceeds autumn but is still very much part of the summer season.

During the hottest days of summer, plants can look as exhausted as I sometimes feel. Their leaves and flowers can droop and their colours look washed out in the strong light. The latter part of summer, however, is different, and it often starts in some gardens with the first flowering of black-eyed Susan (*Rudbeckia*), which heralds a change in the colour palette and also in the mood that pervades the garden.

Ochre is just one of the shades of yellow that steadily begin to dominate the late summer garden. The change is not abrupt as already heliopsis and some cultivars of helenium will have started to flower in mid-summer. When these are joined by daisylike black-eyed Susan, other yellow-flowered daisies arrive as well, including helianthus, more heleniums, coreopsis, and ubiquitous golden rod (*Solidago*). Together these familiar perennials bring a warm, vibrant glow to the late summer garden and reintroduce

Two excellent, rich-toned cultivars of helenium are *Helenium* 'Königstiger' and mellow yellow *H.* 'Zimbelstern'.

the vigour that might otherwise be on the wane in many gardens once the longer days of mid-summer had passed. Invigorated by this new troupe of players, the late summer garden is capable of being developed into a spectacular seasonal theme, which for many gardeners can be the highlight of their gardening year.

The best of the black-eyed Susans for general use is *Rudbeckia fulgida* var. *deamii*, which grows some 1.2m (4ft) tall. This is taller than the better-known *Rudbeckia fulgida* var. *sullivantii* 'Goldsturm', with its slightly lighter yellow petals surrounding the typical, tight, black central cone of the genus. Its extra height helps when it is used in combinations with late-flowering ornamental grasses such as miscanthus and panicum, which are its perfect partners.

Among other splendid members of this genus is *R. laciniata* 'Herbstsonne', which is ideal at the back of borders. It reaches more

than 1.8m (6ft) and has bold yellow flowers with petals that hang down below the central black cone. Even more dramatic is earlier-flowering *R. maxima*, with its flowers that have central cones extended like long hooked fingers. Its large, glaucous-blue basal foliage is another of its characteristics that can play an important role in any planting designs. However, unlike the other black-eyed Susans, this is not an easy plant to grow, as it demands well-drained, fertile soil in an open, uncluttered situation with full sun. By late summer its petals will have fallen, but its black cones and leaves carry the display through into winter.

The character of *R. triloba* is different. It bears the smallest flowers of the genus in great profusion. Plants develop into bushes 1–2m (3–6½ft) tall and flower throughout late summer and autumn. In truth they are short-lived, often surviving just two or three seasons, but they self-seed freely and can be grown as annuals and treated in the same way as lupins (*see p.131*).

Heleniums are favourite perennials of many gardeners. As a traditional member of the herbaceous border they have a long history, and many cultivars have been named. The vigour of some of the older selections is poor and often associated with nematode infections. This explains why sometimes plants fail to grow well. Mostly, however, heleniums are easy tough plants so long as the soil is not too dry and they receive plenty of sun and air. Among the earliest to flower are readily available *H.* 'Moerheim Beauty' and *H.* 'Rubinzwerg', which is less vigorous and more difficult to propagate. Both have rich mahogany-red flowers, although *H.* 'Rubinzwerg' flowers earlier and in a richer red. If you deadhead these plants, they will continue to flower into late summer. Such dark colours bring a strong contrast to the summer border, but if something fresher is needed then *H.* 'Sahin's Early Flowerer' lives up to its rather awkward name. Its orange-streaked flowers become progressively more yellow as they age.

Some people deride heleniums as tall awkward plants with ugly stems, bare at the base. This can be true. Some cultivars are tall and quickly lose their lower leaves, but this drawback can easily be overcome. One method is to position them at the back of a large border with other plants in front; their lower stems will soon be overgrown and

hidden by their neighbours. However, the best way to manage heleniums, and indeed many other tall-growing perennials such as asters, is to prune them.

Heleniums respond well to their shoots being cut back by one-third to one-half once they have reached half their ultimate height. In practice this means that they are pruned in late spring or early summer. Pruning has three noticeable effects: firstly, the plant's ultimate height is reduced, although this can be adjusted by the severity of the cutback; secondly, the start of flowering will be delayed by a couple of weeks; and, thirdly, the number of flowers borne will be greater, though they may be smaller sized. Every stem that is cut back responds by producing two or more side shoots, all of which flower.

Sometimes a more thoughtful pruning treatment is appropriate. For example, if only half of the stems of a clump of helenium are cut back those that remain will flower first, to be followed a couple of weeks later by the rest, thereby prolonging its flowering season. In many cases, every stem can be shortened to some extent in order to reduce the height of the plants and eliminate the need for staking. At other times some stems are cut back harder to further delay their flowering.

In late summer, when so many bright yellow "daisies" are in flower, heleniums with dark-coloured flowers are very useful for contrast and relief. *Helenium* 'Moerheim Beauty' is probably the most popular of these, and has dark mahogany-red petals surrounding each dark brown flower centre. It is of medium height (1m/3ft) and easily grown. Its one disadvantage is that as the flowers age they become browner and paler, which can prove disappointing. For this reason *H.* 'Rubinzwerg' might be a better choice. It is slightly shorter (80cm/32in) and produces flowers that are even richer in colour, yet they do not discolour as badly as those of *H.* 'Moerheim Beauty'. Different but useful in the same way is *H.* 'Karneol', with its soft orange-red flowers, which appear to

Rudbeckia laciniata 'Herbstsonne' is a good choice for a dramatic perennial to place at the very back of a late summer border.

A trial bed of helenium cultivars in my garden is backed by *Eupatorium purpureum* subsp. *maculatum* 'Riesenschirm' and the less well-known, yellow *Senecio doria*. The senecio is a useful perennial for filling the background of larger-scale planting schemes.

glow paler towards the centre; it matures to about 1m (3ft) tall.

Helenium 'Waltraut' is typical of many cultivars with a base colour (here burnt yellow) heavily overlaid and streaked in red or orange. In this case the red-orange colour dominates and becomes more intense as the flowers age. This cultivar is especially valuable since it grows no more than 80cm (32in) tall. At the other end of the height scale is *H.* 'Feuersiegel' at 1.7m (5½ft) tall. Its flowers have a deep yellow base colour and orange-red streaking, which fades slightly as they age. When grown at the very back of the border, *H.* 'Feuersiegel' does not require pruning at all, but some sort of staking will probably prove necessary.

Equally tall with warm yellow petals around contrasting dark brown centres is *H.* 'Pumilum Magnificum', which is among the longest flowering of all the cultivars. Its height is easily manipulated with pruning, making it one of the best. Another excellent helenium is *H.* 'Zimbelstern'. At 1.2m (4ft) it is of a convenient height, and its flowers are soft golden-yellow with a few orange streaks when newly opened. These quickly disappear. The centres of the flowers start green and gradually become light brown, which together with the gentle tint of its petals creates a most natural and harmonious character that blends with almost anything you might think of combining it with. Further good heleniums for the perennial garden include *H.* 'Flammenspiel', *H.* 'Goldfuchs', *H.* 'Goldrausch', *H.* 'Königstiger', and the exciting newer *H.* 'Rauchtopas' with its curved petals showing mahogany-brown on the underside and warm yellow above.

Annual sunflowers (*Helianthus*) are the epitome of summer, but the perennial sorts are far less popular with many gardeners. The reason is that many are coarse in habit and spread aggressively underground. There are two notable examples that should be included in any planting scheme attempting to reach a fiery crescendo in late summer. *Helianthus*

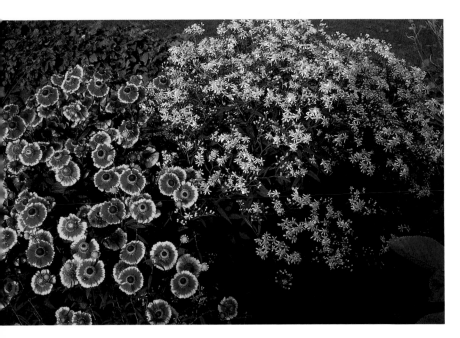

TOP The flower shapes and textures of *Helenium* 'Biedermeier' and *Aster umbellatus* look good at the rear of a border.

ABOVE The rich red flowers of *Helenium* 'Baudirektor Linne' fade to dark rusty orange as they age.

freshness at a time of year when other garden tints are becoming mellow.

In comparison *H. microcephallus* is more subdued – if such a word can be ever applied to a sunflower. Dozens of fine dark stems rise 2m (6½ft) into the air and are covered in medium-sized, dark green, pointed leaves. Until it flowers, it remains unnoticed as a sombre member of the background. In late summer, its dark foliage provides the perfect setting for the single, lemon-yellow flowers. They are small for a sunflower, at around 6cm (2½in) in diameter, yet in scale with any rudbeckias and heleniums nearby. Its wiry upright form never needs staking, and the clumps are compact and generally less than 60cm (2ft) across.

Another columnar plant that is strong and reaches more than 2m (6½ft) at flowering time is *Verbesina alternifolia*. This rarely encountered perennial is far more pleasing than its description can ever suggest. A single plant will make a clump some 60cm (2ft) across after three years, from which its plain green foliage rises. No matter how hard the wind blows, its winged stems never need support. Only the tops of its stems are covered in numerous small, misshapen, light yellow flowers, which are extremely popular with insects. This affable member of the border is always a talking point for gardeners because it brings variety to the mixture of yellows assembled for a bold, late summer display. Ideally *V. alternifolia* should be sited towards the back of a planting scheme.

Coreopsis tripteris is one more suggestion to add to this dramatic group of perennials. It reaches the same proportions as the plants just described, and yet again it is one of those giants that rarely needs support. The plain green stems carry attractive, narrow, pointed leaves, and the flowers are light yellow funnels with a soft brown heart. It is a charming species, and it blends readily with its neighbours.

Contrast with all of these yellow, daisylike flowers is needed in a border design, and

'Lemon Queen' is too large for a small garden but is a wonderful plant when grown in the right place. It makes a tall voluminous clump of fresh green foliage, which reaches 2m (6½ft) by the time of flowering. The single, lemon-yellow flowers are numerous and not more than 8cm (3in) in diameter. *Helianthus* 'Lemon Queen' seems to sparkle with

there are many good perennials to consider for this. Although golden rod is also yellow, *Solidago rugosa* 'Fireworks' has a strikingly different shape. Its name perfectly describes the way the long thin flower spikes arch outwards to create a vigorous horizontal pattern, which is best introduced in the middle or front of a planting scheme.

Although asters are one of the most important planting themes for autumn, some flower much earlier and can bring disparate shapes and colours to your summer designs. For tall, dramatic, late summer borders the wild species *Aster umbellatus* is indispensable. At 1.5m (5ft) high, it can be combined with tall grasses and perennials towards the back of a planting scheme. Its single white flowers have yellow centres and are arranged – as the name suggests – into wide, umbrella-shaped flower heads. Later these form heads of fluffy seeds, which introduce an interesting texture to the autumn garden.

The best-known, summer-flowering asters are cultivars of *A. thomsonii*, *A. amellus*, and the hybrid formed by crossing them, *A. x frikartii*. For mounds of blue at the front of beds and borders they are invaluable. Unfortunately, these are not the easiest of asters to establish and grow, and you might prefer the less formal character of *A. pyrenaeus* 'Lutetia'. It forms loose arching mounds of flowers for weeks on end. These are pale lilac-blue with fine ray petals, some 3cm (1in) across, which belie its toughness and ease of cultivation.

Surprisingly, some asters are useful for dry shady conditions. *Aster macrophyllus* can be invasive in better conditions, but in dry corners of the garden this tendency is tempered and as a result it makes effective groundcover. The less invasive and the even earlier-flowering *A. divaricatus* is a good choice for small gardens. Both species bear fairly similar, small, starlike, white flowers. For such shady situations, you should try the exquisite form of *A. macrophyllus* 'Twilight',

Helianthus microcephallus

with its light blue flowers appearing from summer through to early autumn.

Another member of the daisy family is *Vernonia crinita* 'Mammuth', which grows 2m (6½ft) tall on stiff stems bearing narrow pointed leaves and tight clusters of dark reddish-purple, daisylike flowers. It begins to flower towards the end of summer and continues well into early autumn.

At the back of a border nothing could be better at this time of the year than a large clump of Joe Pye weed (*Eupatorium purpureum*). It reaches 2m (6½ft) tall and comes into flower in mid-summer. However,

it is at its best later, and it remains effective through autumn and winter as a sturdy silhouette. The rounded clusters of purple flowers are larger than a football, providing bulk and colour. Even grown as specimens, these plants are worthwhile, but their shape and form suggest many combinations, especially with the taller-growing ornamental grasses. Various cultivars exist but their differences are often hard to see as the plant's size and vigour vary so much depending on soil fertility and moisture.

In America the standard form of Joe Pye weed is *E. purpureum* subsp. *maculatum*

BELOW The flowers of *Filipendula rubra* 'Venusta' are like frothy pink candyfloss in early summer. They fade quickly and go on to make ginger-toned seed heads that remain effective at the back of borders for months. They are seen here in the company of eupatorium.

'Gateway' and in Europe it is *E.p.* subsp. *maculatum* 'Atropurpureum'. You might, however, prefer *E.p.* subsp. *maculatum* 'Glutball', because the flower colour is slightly more intense. For the tallest selection of all, look out for *E.p.* subsp. *maculatum* 'Riesenschirm'. Shorter-growing cultivars such as *E.p.* 'Purple Bush' are hardly any lower than the species, while the white-flowered ones, such as *E.p.* subsp. *maculatum* 'Album' and *E.p.* 'Bartered Bride', are extremely tall but have an inherent problem because when the flowers fade they begin to turn a dirty shade of brown.

RIGHT *Solidago rugosa* 'Fireworks' has its flowers arranged in a highly effective pattern, which is ideal for setting up contrasts with nearby verticals in planting schemes.

BELOW *Aster umbellatus* is more often seen at the back of a border, but here it performs gracefully along with *Persicaria amplexicaulis* 'Speciosum' in a narrow sunny border.

FURTHER SUMMER-FLOWERING PERENNIALS

Aruncus
Height of foliage: 70–90cm (28–36in)
Height in flower: 1–1.5m (3–5ft)
Tolerates most growing conditions, including dry shade.
Aruncus flowers in early summer before the bulk of
extravagant, more colourful perennials. Low-growing
A. aethusifolius has attractive, glossy, yellow-green
foliage below upright spikes of off-white flowers.
Unquestionably the best of the new race of its hybrids is
A. 'Horatio', which is distinctly different from the more
familiar species and cultivars, reaching 1.3m (4¼ft) tall
in fertile soils. A. dioicus 'Zweiweltenkind', at 1.5m
(5ft), has graceful, open, clean, white flower heads.

Astilbe chinensis var. taquetii 'Purpurlanze'
Height of foliage: 40cm (16in)
Height in flower: 90cm (36in)
Tolerates drier and sunnier conditions than most astilbes.
This vigorous plant has pale green, divided foliage. Its
stiff habit gives A. chinensis var. taquetii 'Purpurlanze'
a strong architectural character, which can be used to
create lines and bold drifts amid looser-growing plants.
From mid-summer its rich and intense, purple-pink hue
shines out – too strongly for some. The brown seed
heads remain effective for months.

Astrantia
Height of foliage: 30cm (12in)
Height in flower: 60cm (24in)
Prefers humus-rich, moist soils in sun or partial shade.
Originally, astrantias had pale off-white to pink flowers
and were associated with cottage gardens. A. major
subsp. involucrata 'Canneman' and A.m. subsp.
involucrata 'Shaggy' are two good examples of such
plants, while A. 'Buckland' has large, pale pink flowers.
More recently dark red forms have become popular.
A. major 'Claret' is a dark red cultivar grown from
seed collected from the smaller-growing A.m. 'Ruby
Wedding'. Slightly taller-growing A. 'Hadspen Blood'
bears even darker flowers on almost black stems.

Echinacea purpurea
Height of foliage: 30cm (12in)
Height in flower: 1m (3ft)
Needs fertile, well-drained soil that remains so through
winter. Only in open, sunny sites is it reliably perennial.
Coneflowers (E. purpurea) are fantastic for creating
a summer theme. Good, purple-coloured cultivars
include E.p. 'Augustkönigin', E.p. 'Ruby Giant', and
E.p. 'Rubinstern' with larger than average, deep-toned
flowers. There are whites such as E.p. 'White Swan',
and now new forms are appearing in lemon-yellow
(E.p. 'Sunset') and shades of orange (E.p. 'Art's Pride').
These prairie plants seem intolerant of competition and
may not prove long-lived in densely planted borders. If
they grow well for you they should be used extensively
as they flower throughout summer and their central
cones remain as ornamental features into winter.

Hemerocallis
Height of foliage: 40–70cm (16–28in)
Height in flower: 50–90cm (20–36in)
Grows readily in most soils, so long as they are not too
dry, in full sun or partial shade.
Daylilies (Hemerocallis) start into growth in early
spring when their bright fresh foliage can become an
important design feature in its own right. They flower in
summer, and their season can be extended significantly

ABOVE LEFT Hemerocallis
and heleniums

ABOVE Aruncus 'Horatio'

BELOW Astrantia 'Buckland'

by deadheading. In shades of yellow and terracotta they can establish a bold colour theme that can eventually be taken over in late summer by heleniums, rudbeckias, and sunflowers.

Monarda
Height of foliage: 30–80cm (12–32in)
Height in flower: 0.8–1.6m (32–64in)
Tolerates any garden soil and sun or partial shade, but drought curtails its flowering season and leads to powdery mildew infestations that defoliate plants. These essential perennials for summer borders have the bonus of a bold winter aspect. Many modern cultivars of bergamots (*Monarda*) are more resistant to mildew than the older ones. Some of the best are: *M.* 'Aquarius', 1.3m (4¼ft), light violet-purple flowers; the old but relatively healthy *M.* 'Beauty of Cobham', 1.2m (4ft), light pink flowers with dark bracts; *M.* 'Cherokee', 1.6m (5¼ft), pink with a green heart and brown bracts; *M.* 'Scorpion', 1.4m (4½ft), clear violet with dark bracts; and *M.* 'Squaw', 1.2m (4ft), pure red flowers.

Persicaria polymorpha
Height of foliage: 1.5m (5ft)
Height in flower: 1.7m (5½ft)
Prefers rich moist soil in full sun or partial shade sheltered from buffeting winds.
This giant perennial grows quickly during spring and starts producing its creamy white flowers in early summer. It will still have flowers in late summer but by then they will be far less noticeable. The plants die down in autumn and should be cleared away as they have no winter aspect.

Phlomis
Height of foliage: 30–70cm (12–28in)
Height in flower: 0.8–1.6m (32–64in)
Most species require open, sunny, well-drained soil. *P. russeliana* (80cm/32in) has ground-smothering rosettes of yellow-green, hairy leaves through which upright flower stems develop in early summer. The pale yellow flowers are arranged in wreaths around the stems at regular intervals to create a strongly architectural form that remains effective through into winter as the seed heads form. *P. tuberosa* 'Amazone' is much taller (1.6m/64in) and slimmer, with small, lilac-pink flowers arranged in a similar pattern up its stems.

Phlox
Height of foliage: to 30cm (12in)
Height in flower: 0.9–1.8m (36–72in)
Requires moist, fertile, humus-rich soil in full sun or partial shade.
Billowing masses of phlox flowers in mid-summer make the perfect foil for roses and any other pastel-tinted flowers. *P. paniculata* comes in a wide range of colours but all too often the plants are martyrs to disease and infestation. Two of the cultivars selected by Coen Jansen are free from mildew and sturdy enough not to need staking: *P.p.* 'Hesperis', 1.4m (4½ft), is an intense magenta-pink; and *P.p* 'Utopia', to 1.8m (6ft), has large, pale pink flowers with a flush of lilac in late summer. The nearest to blue is *P.p.* 'Blue Paradise'. In hot sunshine it is violet-mauve, but in cool weather and in the evening it becomes indigo-blue. *P. maculata* is lower growing and earlier flowering than *P. paniculata* cultivars. The flowers are arranged in pyramidal clusters. Pink *P. maculata* 'Alpha' and white, lilac-eyed *P.m.* 'Omega' are easy, disease-free cultivars.

Thalictrum
Height of foliage: 50–60cm (20–24in)
Height in flower: 1.8m (6ft)
Prefers well-drained soil that does not dry out in summer; needs a sheltered, partially shaded site. The violet-purple flowers of *T. rochebruneanum* are held in an open flower head by a thick stiff stem above the dark-tinted foliage. Given room and light to develop properly this species does not need staking. *T. lucidum* has green-yellow flowers, while *T. pubescens* is sturdy and has white flowers over well-branched flower heads. *T. delavayi* 'Ankum' reaches 2m (6½ft) tall and bears intensely violet-purple, elegant flowers that need some support if they are to stand up straight.

Thalictrum delavayi **'Ankum'**

BELOW LEFT *Phlomis russeliana*

BELOW *Monarda* 'Aquarius'

Autumn

ABOVE Upright *Miscanthus sinensis* 'Ghana', seen here with *Aster* 'Coombe Fishacre', is one of the most spectacular varieties of miscanthus to develop autumn tints.

LEFT Plumes of *Miscanthus sinensis* 'Kleine Fontäne' create a fine background for the rich tones of *Dahlia* 'Fire Mountain', *Aster cordifolius* 'Ideal', *A.* 'Coombe Fishacre', and a short pruned plant of blue *A.* 'Little Carlow' on the right. *Aster* 'Pink Star' is also to be seen in the background.

Many of the plants that were stars in high summer may continue flowering in autumn, when temperatures begin to fall and day lengths shorten ever further. Although less abundant, flowers will still appear on the clan of yellow "daisies" such as the rudbeckias, helianthus, heliopsis, and coreopsis, which harmonize readily with the mellowing tones that gradually begin to surround them. Other remnants of summer can also add diversity to your planting schemes: for example, heleniums, lupins, delphiniums, and other "earlies" that were cut back at once after their first flowering in summer in the hope that they may start to produce flowers again.

Yet another group of perennials, having begun to bloom many weeks earlier, seem to gather strength in autumn. The rightful season for *Anemone* x *hybrida* is autumn, yet they may start to flower in late summer. Their clumps become covered in a mass of blooms, bringing white and shades of pink into the garden, including into the most inhospitable corners. Some varieties of *Persicaria amplexicaulis* flower in mid-summer. Often, if the ensuing summer is hot and dry, they then seem to hesitate and flowering becomes thinner. However, once into autumn the plants pick up, flowering increases, and as temperatures begin to drop the flower colour of many of the red cultivars intensifies. Thus, by continuing to provide bold colour and distinctive flower patterns in the garden right up until the first frosts of winter, *P. amplexicaulis* earns itself an indispensable place in a bed or border.

The differing characteristics of aster species, including *Aster laevis*, *A. novae-angliae*, and *A. ericoides*, have combined here to build an impressive autumn scene.

Planting Themes of Autumn

Officially autumn starts when day and night are of equal length at the autumn equinox, but for gardeners the beginning of the season is more likely to be signalled by asters finally coming into flower.

Asters offer the last big chance of the year to flood the garden with flower colour, but they do have a bad reputation. This goes back to the mildew-ridden spreaders which were disparagingly referred to as michaelmas daisies. In the main these were cultivars, or more likely self-seedlings, of the *Aster novi-*

belgii group with washed-out, mauve-tinted flowers. Nothing could be more different from the stars of my autumn garden, the thought of which makes me look forward to this late season with anticipation and longing even in the heady days of summer.

There is far more to asters than the ubiquitous cultivars of *A. novi-belgii* and New England aster (*A. novae-angliae*). Not all asters spread aggressively into neighbouring plants nor do they all suffer from mildew. Many of the species asters are graceful and elegant and carry small delicate flowers. They are adaptable plants that respond to pruning to reduce their height where necessary and to reduce the need for staking. They are also tolerant of a wide range of growing conditions.

Aster umbellatus has already been encountered as one of the essential components at the back of a herbaceous border (*see p.149*). It flowers in late summer with flat-topped clusters of yellow-centred, white flowers, but in autumn these transform into fluffy, off-white clouds of seed that remain a positive and attractive feature for many weeks.

Asters generally need full sun to retain a compact habit and to flower profusely; however, a few species are an exception to this rule and therefore very useful. They flower earlier in the year than the bulk of the autumn-flowering asters. I grow *A. divaricatus* where it will bring a drift of white flowers to an area of shade created by a tall clump of aruncus. It grows 45cm (18in) tall and spreads steadily, but not aggressively, into wide horizontal clumps, which come into flower in mid- to late summer and continue to make a gentle contribution for more than a month.

Aster macrophyllus has a wilder character that looks at home in the inhospitable conditions of dry shade. Here, its aggressive nature is held in check, but it survives, making broad, coarse-leaved groundcover and in late summer sends up stiff open flower heads of fine-petalled flowers. Individually the flowers are unexciting, but en masse the effect is pleasing, especially in places where otherwise there would be nothing. A far more attractive plant, clearly closely related to it, is *A.m.* 'Twilight'. The foliage is not so coarse, and the pale lilac-blue flowers bring colour to shady corners even when the soil is dry. In better conditions, it will spread quickly and needs watching, but for the clear colour of its flowers alone it is definitely worth growing.

Cultivars of *A. ericoides* are also remarkably tolerant of dry conditions and rarely suffer from mildew; they make informal mounds of fine-leaved foliage and in mid-autumn cover themselves in hundreds of tiny single flowers. Of these *A.e.* 'Pink Cloud' and *A.e.* 'Blue Star', both growing 80cm (32in) tall, are worthwhile and *A.e.* 'Golden Spray', the white-flowered cultivar with bright yellow centres to its flower, is useful almost anywhere in a border. My only reservation with this group is that their flowers can be easily ruined by night frosts. When they

escape this fate their billowing clouds of misty colour combine very well with grassy foliage. However, as their contribution to a garden can too frequently be cut short you might wish to seek alternatives.

Aster cordifolius tolerates light shade and dryish soil, but only flowers well when the soil is humus rich and moisture retentive. There are a few cultivars with attractive single flowers such as *A.c.* 'Ideal' in pale lilac and the slightly taller *A.c.* 'Sweet Lavender', at 1.2m (4ft). One that is said to be the tallest is called *A.c.* 'Chieftain'; it produces rich clear blue flowers on plants to 1.5m (5ft) tall.

Two hybrids with *A. cordifolius* in their parentage are probably my favourite of all asters because of their clear flower colour and long flowering season. *Aster* 'Little Carlow' is indispensable. Its 3cm (1in) wide flowers are clear lavender-blue and held in sturdy upright branches. Its flower heads are so full that they do need some support, but this is a

The vibrant hues of *Aster novae-angliae* 'Andenken an Alma Pötschke' and the paler *A. n.-a.* 'Harrington's Pink' behind contrast with the backlit flower heads of *Miscanthus sinensis* 'Grosse Fontäne' and the autumn tints in the foliage of *Rhus* x *pulvinata* Autumn Lace Group ('syn. *R. glabra* 'Laciniata').

small price to pay for a display that goes on undiminished for a month, sometimes starting in the very earliest weeks of autumn.

Another favourite, *A.* 'Photograph', bears many more flowers but they are only 1.5cm (½in) across in a paler, less insistent tone of lavender-blue. In appearance, *A.* 'Photograph' resembles *A. ericoides* but the habit is more open and airy, and it grows taller. Again, some support is advisable to prevent the stems flopping over neighbouring plants. The clumps do not increase in size very quickly. In spring *A.* 'Photograph' is susceptible to slug attack. However, it is worth the effort of protecting and nurturing such a fine plant.

Aster 'Pink Star' has compact, fine-leaved clumps growing 1.2m (4ft) tall. For weeks on end they are covered with 1cm (⅜in) wide, purple-pink, single flowers. This is an easy plant to slip in between other perennials in a border, where it remains unnoticed for most of the year. In late summer it rises up through its neighbours to start flowering at the dawn

of autumn, and it can be relied on to be effective well into mid-autumn.

The tallest asters can hold their own among miscanthus grasses. The wild species *A. laevis* has wiry stems and small, dark green leaves. In mid-autumn it bears tiny, starry, blue flowers. At more than 2m (6½ft) tall it weaves itself among the tallest grasses at the back of borders. A better plant is *A.l.* 'Calliope', with its small, leathery, dark green leaves sparsely held on dark stems that are reminiscent of some black-stemmed bamboos. The 3cm (1in) wide, lilac-purple flowers open over an airy flower head. Another cultivar, *A.l.* 'Blauschleier', with its clear blue flowers is more easily accommodated, growing only 1.5m (5ft) tall. Recently introduced *A.l.* 'Anneke van der Jeugd' is an improved form with a longer flowering season. The only drawback with *A. laevis* and its cultivars is the need to stake the plants, even when earlier in the season their woody habit suggests that this might not be necessary.

The numerous cultivars of *Miscanthus sinensis* spread throughout my own garden serve to unite it into a single planting scheme during late autumn.

Exciting autumn theme plantings can be created when a varied selection of the asters mentioned so far are mixed together and repeated through all of the borders of the same garden to unite it into a crescendo of seasonal colour.

Some species of aster require excellent drainage and considerable sunshine. Also, they can only be planted in spring since a long wet winter following an autumn planting will invariably kill them. The smallest-growing of these is *A. thomsonii* 'Nanus'. It has lavender-blue flowers covering its neat, 30cm (1ft) mounds of foliage from late summer through to mid-autumn, and even on into winter some years.

The 5cm (2in) wide flowers of *A. amellus* are slightly larger with twice as many broader petals – or more accurately ray florets. The rich violet and purple colours displayed by the various cultivars create bold splashes of colour from late summer onwards. The cultivar *A.a.* 'Veilchenkönigin' can be difficult to grow on heavy clay soil. *A.a.* 'Gründer', however, is bigger and stronger in every way and should be easier to please.

Aster x *frikartii* – the hybrid created between *A. thomsonii* and *A. amellus* – is far better known and often touted as one of the best hardy perennials of all. However, it is available in only a limited number of cultivars. Four of these are the result of crosses made by the Swiss nurseryman Frikart in 1918 and 1924: *A.* x *f.* 'Mönch', *A.* x *f.* 'Wunder von Stäfa', *A.* x *f.* 'Jungfrau', and *A.* x *f.* 'Eiger'. The first two are almost identical, and the last two are more compact, less likely to need staking, and are also difficult to distinguish from one another. On balance, *A.* x *f.* 'Jungfrau' is the one to grow. Another cross was made by Alan Bloom of England's Bressingham Nurseries in 1964. Called *A.* x *f.* 'Flora's Delight', it is sturdy and compact, growing only 45cm (18in) high, and is probably the best of the bunch.

The one thing that all of the asters described so far have in common is their delicacy and informality, which means they are easy to blend with other plants in the garden. Their colours are harmonious shades of pink, blue, lavender, violet, and purple, but none of them could ever be labelled strident or dominating. When in mid-autumn asters are in flower throughout a garden – at the front, in the middle, and at the back of every border – the effect is that of a mist of pastel tints seeming to swirl and drift, and it seems capable of engulfing the entire space.

If asters are planted together with flowering grasses, an image may be created of a foam-tipped ocean whipped up by tempestuous winds. Such a theme can be used to unite different parts of a garden into a single entity. By then, the plants it contains will have matured, and autumn tints will already be spreading through their thinning foliage. The asters will have done their work by winter, shades of brown and straw may fill every corner of the garden, and all that will remain will be the silhouettes of perennials to carry memories of the recent past through into a new growing year.

Autumn Tints and Silhouettes

In autumn, deciduous plants drop their leaves, the garden's framework thins, and any perennials that leave behind seed heads and stems create a matrix of textures and muted tints. Bold clumps of eupatoriums are reduced to stiff blackened stems topped by the silhouettes of their former, dome-shaped flower heads. The upright flower spikes of veronicas turn into chocolate-coloured seed heads. The black centres of rudbeckia flowers and the central cones of echinaceas remain at the end of bare stems to resemble drumsticks, while the seed-head blobs of monardas and crooked fingers of sanguisorbas seem to function as full stops and commas through the texture pictures that become the persistent images of autumn.

Sedum spectabile and *S. telephium* flower in late summer, as do their cultivars and many related hybrids such as *S.* 'Purple Emperor', *S.* 'Abbeydore', and *S.* 'Karfunkelstein'. By autumn their congested flower heads in shades of pink and red have faded and turned into solid domes of dark brown. These function as rounded boulders at the edge of a stream,

containing and contrasting with wispier plant material in the background.

Late-flowering grasses, which dominate summer borders, continue to be effective in autumn. Miscanthus flower heads once tinted in shades of pink and gold become frothy white. Steadily their foliage begins to pale, acquiring washes of yellow and ochre before eventually becoming as bleached as straw.

The fountainlike foliage and flower heads of molinias are bright green through summer but go a vibrant shade of golden-yellow in autumn. This seems to accentuate their presence within a planting scheme as if they were being picked out by a spotlight. Panicums and sorghastrum, likewise, turn from grey-green to yellow, and ground-covering *Hakonechloa macra* changes into a warm shade of light tan. Other perennials develop rich autumn tints before dropping their foliage. For example, *Gillenia trifoliata* turns rich shades of russet, hostas become amber, and *Euphorbia palustris* and amsonia radiate bright yellow. When low-angled sunlight hits such mellow autumn tints it ignites them into a glorious glittering inferno.

RIGHT The flowers and seed heads of *Actaea simplex* Atropurpurea Group 'James Compton' and *Aster* 'Pink Star' are even more eye-catching when backed by plumes of *Miscanthus sinensis* 'Kleine Fontäne'. The flowers of the grass *Calamagrostis brachytricha* fill the foreground.

BELOW LEFT The fluffy seed heads of *Eupatorium purpureum* eventually look like fine black silhouettes.

BELOW Many sedum seed heads become rich brown in autumn and harden so they last well throughout the winter months.

TOP *Actaea simplex* Atropurpurea Group 'James Compton'

ABOVE *Aster novae-angliae* 'Andenken an Alma Pötschke'

BELOW *Chrysanthemum* 'Herbstbrokat' and the autumn tints of *Gillenia trifoliata*.

FURTHER AUTUMN-FLOWERING PERENNIALS

Aconitum

Height of foliage: 60cm (2ft)
Height in flower: 1.2–1.5m (4–5ft)
Prefers humus-rich, moist but well-drained soil in sun. *A. carmichaelii* Wilsonii Group 'Spätlese' has clear sky-blue flowers arranged in short branching flower spikes in early and mid-autumn. It reaches more than 1.6m (5¼ft) tall when grown in rich soil. *A.c.* Wilsonii Group 'Barker's Variety' starts to flower a few weeks earlier, and its numerous flower spikes are covered in deep mid-blue, hooded blooms. It is a slightly taller and far more dominant plant, and is too heavy for a small garden. However, it is majestic in grander settings.

Actaea

Height of foliage: 70cm (28in)
Height in flower: 1.5–2m (5–6½ft)
Tolerates shade, but needs sun to fully display the dark-leaved forms; requires moist soil in the growing season. Following reclassification, this genus now contains the bugbanes (*Cimicifuga*), an important group of late-flowering woodland plants. These are mound-forming perennials with attractive divided leaves. The flower spikes rise well clear of the foliage and are covered along their length with small white flowers. In early and mid-autumn *A. matsumurae* 'Elstead Variety' (syn. *Cimicifuga simplex* var. *matsumurae* 'Elstead') bears its pink buds, which open into creamy white flowers with pink stamens. The flower stems and fine foliage are slightly tinted purple, unlike two other even later flowering actaeas: *A. simplex* 'Prichard's Giant' and *A. matsumurae* 'White Pearl'.
Dark purple leaf coloration has become a goal in breeding cultivars of *A. simplex*: *A.s.* Atropurpurea Group 'Brunette', which was one of the first of these to appear, is relatively compact, no more than 1.5m (5ft) in flower, with black-brown foliage and scented flowers, which attract numerous insects. *A.s.* Atropurpurea Group 'James Compton' has a more metallic sheen to its foliage and is the tallest selection so far, at nearly 2m (6½ft) when in flower. These are slow-growing plants that will take 2–3 years to establish and develop into significant clumps.

Anemone

Height of foliage: 60cm (2ft)
Height in flower: 1.2m (4ft)
Partial shade is ideal; tolerates dry conditions once established; can be invasive in humus-rich, moist soils. Without doubt, *A. x hybrida* 'Honorine Jobert' is the best, white, autumn-flowering anemone. Its single white flowers with yellow stamens are held above bold, jagged, dark green foliage. Like many other cultivars,

these plants take a few years to settle into a new planting site, but thereafter they grow vigorously and flower profusely. *A. x h.* 'Königin Charlotte' and *A. x h.* 'September Charm' are two good pink varieties. Lower-growing *A. hupehensis* has yielded some valuable border plants, of which *A. x hybrida* 'Lady Gilmour' (syn. *A. hupehensis* 'Crispa') is unique. The violet-pink flowers are a bonus as it is for the frilly edged leaves that this plant is generally grown. They are light green and full of texture. *A. hupehensis* 'Hadspen Abundance' is a perfect, front-of-border plant with two-tone, pink blooms no more than 50cm (20in) tall.

Aster

Height of foliage: 40–60cm (16–24in)
Height in flower: 0.8–1.7m (32–68in)
Thrives in sun and fertile, well-drained soil with some exceptions.
In addition to the species described on pp.156–9, the most commonly encountered asters are cultivars of New England aster (*A. novae-angliea*) and New York aster or Michaelmas daisy (*A. novi-belgii*). They offer a wide range of flower colours with both single- and double-flowered forms, but many gardeners find them difficult to grow. Many are prone to disease, some spread aggressively, and all need replanting every two to three years to give of their best. However, as with any generalization, there will always be exceptions. *A. novi-belgii* 'Chequers' makes a compact clump 60cm (2ft) tall, with narrow, dark green foliage. The sumptuously coloured flowers are deep violet-purple set off by bright yellow disc florets at their centres. *A. n-b.* 'Chequers' is free from mildew. Frustratingly, its clumps are very slow to enlarge and offer material for propagation. *A. novae-angliae* 'Harrington's Pink' is far more typical of its type, being 1.5m (5ft) tall, with ugly stems that become bare at the base and coarse, pale green foliage. It retains its position in the garden because of its flower colour, which is the clearest glowing pink imaginable.
A shorter, equally desirable plant is *A. n-a.* 'Andenken an Alma Pötschke'. The growth habit is more compact, and the vivid, cerise-pink flowers are darker.

Chrysanthemum

Height of foliage: 60cm (24in)
Height in flower: 70cm (28in)
Prefers fertile calcareous soils; heavy clay soils and winter damp will lead to losses. Grow in full sun and protect the roots in cold, exposed situations. For late-season colour chrysanthemums offer an alternative to the more dominant asters, but they lack sufficient character to be considered as a major theme plant in my perennial borders. *C.* 'Bronze Elegance' and

C. 'Herbstbrokat' bear small, double, pompom flowers in a medley of orange and brown very late in the year. Sometimes, they flower so late that they are caught by frost before having time to enrich nearby autumn tints. C. 'Anja's Bouquet' likewise makes useful rounded clumps of attractive green foliage, some 70cm (28in) tall. It bears pink flowers. Others such as C. 'Anastasia' and C. 'Emperor of China' might be considered worth including in the border, in order to cling on to the last drops of colour that a garden can offer.

Leucanthemella serotina (syn. *Chrysanthemum uliginosum*)

Height of foliage: 50–60cm (20–24in)
Height in flower: 1.7–2m (5½–6½ft)

Occurs naturally beside ponds and streams so needs soil that does not dry out; does tolerate well-drained but moist soil. Full exposure to sun prevents these tall plants from leaning towards the light.

This significant plant grows up to 2m (6½ft) tall with single, white, yellow-centred, daisy-like flowers. The colour harmonizes well with yellows such as rudbeckias, heliopsis, and verbesina. It flowers from late summer on into autumn and makes a fine backdrop to a border filled with lower-growing, pastel-tinted asters. The flowers of *L. serotina* always face the sun so it should be placed carefully; staking will also be necessary, but otherwise this is an easy-going, hardy perennial.

Persicaria amplexicaulis

Height of foliage: 60–90cm
Height in flower: 90–120cm

Grows readily in sunny and partially shaded situations in garden soils that do not dry out in summer.

P. amplexicaulis is available in a number of outstanding cultivar forms, which are effective from mid-summer to the first frosts of winter. They make impressive, wide-spreading clumps of coarse, mid-green foliage above which slim flower spikes rise, creating bulk and vertical accents at the front or side of a border. At one time there were only three cultivars of *P. amplexicaulis*: *P.a.* 'Alba', which bears subtle, slightly twisted, wispy flower spikes; *P.a.* 'Rosea', which has pink flowers around a dark purple-red stem; and *P.a.* 'Firetail', which produces rich purple-red flower spikes that seem to get more intensely coloured as summer moves into the chill of autumn. There are now many more persicarias offering different tones of flower colour and/or a more compact growth habit: for example, *P.a.* 'Red Baron' is a good deep red and lower growing, to around 80cm (32in); and *P.a.* 'Summer Dance' is a strong pink halfway in tone between *P.a.* 'Firetail' and *P.a.* 'Rosea'.

Sedum

Height of foliage: 30–40cm (12–16in)
Height in flower: 50cm (20in)

Prefers sunny, well-drained soil, but tolerates drought and even damp soil.

S. 'Herbstfreude' (syn. *S.* 'Autumn Joy') is the best known of the group of large perennial sedums used to bring a contrasting form to the front of herbaceous borders. Their thick rounded leaves are effective from the moment they emerge in late spring. During summer, dome-shaped flower heads form; they are green at first, and look like a tasty vegetable. In late summer the flowers open in shades of red, pink, or white over many weeks, but even when these fade to dark shades of brown in autumn they continue to provide bold contrast with any lighter, more upright plant material nearby. *S. telephium* 'Matrona' has proved a great success with gardeners seeking a dark-leaved sedum that provides bold contrast in a planting scheme. Its thick fleshy leaves are pewter-purple all summer, and the strongly shaped flower heads enhance its presence later in the season. While *S.* 'Purple Emperor' offers darker rich purple leaves, it is lower growing, rather straggly, and far less effective. The foliage of *S* 'Karfunkelstein' is a harmonious shade of light purple-grey. It is lower growing than *S. telephium* 'Matrona', which could be a disadvantage, but its flowers still offer good colour and form later in its long effective season. *S.* 'Abbeydore' has glaucous green leaves. Its numerous, relatively small flower heads are light pink maturing to rich red before finally turning brown; often all three stages are to be seen mixed together in the same flower head.

BELOW LEFT *Persicaria amplexicaulis*

BELOW *Sedum* 'Abbeydore'

Planting Themes

Entrance Gardens

LEFT A traditional box parterre makes an appropriate setting for the cottage-style architecture of this British home. It is interplanted with *Allium hollandicum*, here looking regal in early summer. Yellow *Euphorbia characias* together with white and pink forms of valerian (*Centranthus ruber*) enjoy the shelter of the sun-baked conditions below the house's front wall.

A garden in front of your home or a building is a functional space through which you and visitors must pass. I recall a house with a gate in a side street; it was necessary to walk back along its side and across a small patio to reach the front door. The route was beautifully planted, but what an irritation if you had to use it regularly. Practical considerations should be paramount when designing such spaces, but this does not mean that you should not also take the opportunity to express yourself.

The two examples of front gardens on these pages show how different settings and the architecture of the buildings themselves can influence the design approach. In the first, the vernacular façade has been reflected in a traditional box parterre, clipped and ordered, with perennials used within its framework to bring decoration and colour as a gift of welcome to its visitors. The planting in front of the Minimalist American home is an

extension of its architectural style, and directs access (to the front door). Both approaches are valid, as they reflect the personal choices of the respective owners.

Such spaces need not only to look good but also to provide a convenient approach. Paths should lead logically to their destinations, and any planting should reinforce this and not detract or get in the way. Evergreen groundcover is especially useful, being effective all year – unlike many other perennials. In America *Liriope muscari* is very popular, although it may not be hardy enough in some areas. Its dense even habit can effectively be used to line paths and fill in spaces where people should not walk. In late summer it produces attractive spikes of violet-purple flower that elevate its status above more conventional, shrubby groundcover that could be used, such as ivy and box.

Bergenias, euphorbias, epimediums, and many other groundcover plants could function

PREVIOUS PAGES Many perennials relish the damp soil beside natural water features, while true aquatics such as water lilies and marginal plants including certain irises grow with their roots fully submerged. The pink-flowered *Astrantia major* in the foreground flourishes in a wide range of soils so long as they do not dry out; however the double, white-flowered *Ranunculus aconitifolius* 'Flore Pleno' can only thrive, as here, in soil at the water's edge.

RIGHT Architectural clumps of *Pycnanthemum muticum* anchor this Minimalist building to its location both visually and by way of the fact that the plants are native to eastern North America.

LEFT The coastal location of this Maryland residence calls for an informal shingle path with loose drifts of native grasses and perennials reinforcing the relaxed atmosphere.

RIGHT This visitor's cottage – also in Maryland – acquires privacy by the light screen provided by *Molinia caerulea* subsp. *arundinacea*.

in the same way, but perennials can contribute far more than just groundcover. In flower they bring colour and interest, to create a focus of attention. You can use them to enhance the appearance of your home as well as go further than mere decoration by utilizing them to send a message. This could be sober and respectable, in keeping with the tone of the area, but you may also want to take the opportunity to welcome your guests, bid them a fond farewell, and reflect the changing seasons in the one part of your garden that people pass through possibly more than any other.

Ornamental grasses have played an important role in my front gardens ever since I saw a photograph of a garden designed by Wolfgang Oehme and James van Sweden some 20 years ago. A slightly curved path led to the front door and on either side were clumps of tall molinia, panicum, and miscanthus grasses, with their flower heads spread wide, amid simple drifts of colourful perennials such as yellow rudbeckias and dark pink sedums. Swaying in the wind, these flower stems seemed to be there to wave a welcome or bid a farewell in the true spirit of open hospitality.

Groundcover

Alchemilla mollis is one of the most useful perennials for groundcover. After flowering in early summer it should be sheared back to encourage fresh leaves, which will remain attractive for the rest of the growing season.

With a little imagination, groundcover can mean any plants that work well when mass planted and not simply the conventional planting of low-growing evergreens. The term groundcover, however, can take on a negative meaning when garden owners in search of a low-maintenance solution employ contractors who plant wide drifts of geraniums or ivy.

There is nothing wrong with such plants, but when used in such a utilitarian way they have no opportunity to excite your senses or engage your fantasies.

The best plants to use as groundcover are those that mesh together when closely planted and thereby suppress weeds. This is a practical necessity if you are to avoid extra maintenance, yet it should not really be the reason for growing such plants in the first place. The real role of groundcover in the garden is either to create an open space within your planting design or in some way to edge or contain existing planting areas.

Evergreen perennials are particularly effective in the winter garden when they are placed on the corners of flower borders and when used to line paths and axes. From a distance they serve to emphasize the garden's design when the other plants have either died down or lost their leaves. Low box hedges have been used in a similar way for centuries.

The bergenias wrapped around the edges of Beth Chatto's island beds are a good example of the successful planting of ground-covering perennials. Within my own garden, I use crisp lines of low-growing *Euphorbia amygdaloides* var. *robbiae* to edge a central herbaceous border which in spring is filled with tulips and later with perennials but in winter contains nothing apart from dried stems and seed heads. This low-growing euphorbia bears glossy dark green leaves all year. In spring its frothy yellow flower heads, some 55cm (22in) tall, are important, while in winter its lustrous foliage makes a clear contrast with the straw-coloured stems of the dormant perennials and grasses behind it.

Plants that spread out as they grow either underground or with surface-rooting shoots smother the ground and suppress weeds.

Some plants are better at this than others: for example, not all bergenias make good groundcover. Thus, *Bergenia purpurascens* holds its leaves upright instead of making conventional horizontal rosettes. These and any plants struggling to grow well will allow weed seedlings to invade their clumps if they are not carefully tended.

On a smaller scale, but comparable in design terms, is the truly weed-suppressing evergreen *Ajuga reptans*. This is best in bright places on the edge of woodland, where the soil remains reasonably moist all year, and so is not suitable for the gravel garden. Its spreading runners can easily overrun weaker neighbours, but that after all is what is required of effective groundcover. In late spring *A. reptans* bear sprays of blue flowers rising 20–30cm (8–12in) above their ground-hugging foliage. These are a bonus, as it is for its foliage effect that this evergreen perennial is chosen. *Ajuga reptans* 'Atropurpurea' is the common, purple-leaved form, but *A.r.* 'Braunherz' is an improvement,

ABOVE Ornamental grasses (here *Deschampsia cespitosa* 'Goldtau') make good groundcover in a wide range of growing conditions.

LEFT Evergreen bergenias effectively define a bend in the path within this woodland garden.

with much darker and slightly larger leaves. *Ajuga reptans* 'Catlins Giant' lives up to its name – its leaves being twice the size. Unfortunately the foliage is not so richly tinted, more a dark green with irregular, dark brown patches. *Ajuga reptans* 'Grey Lady' has soft grey leaves that might be used to bring light into a shady corner, but to some it looks terribly similar to a mildew-infected ajuga that is being grown in too dry a situation. My all-time favourite here is *A.r.* 'Burgundy Glow', with its dark purple foliage suffused with pink and magenta. It is one plant that is guaranteed to appeal to children of all ages.

Ajuga pyramidalis is also worth seeking out, although it does not spread as vigorously as good groundcover should. Its clumps of leaves are plain dark green, but its flowers are its redeeming factor. Pyramids are far too squat to describe the neat flower spikes of *A. pyramidalis*, so perhaps blue pagodas would be a better epithet.

In any woodland garden, epimediums should be playing an important role as groundcover. Their slowly creeping roots throw up sheaths of exquisite, delicate foliage,

which depending on the species may be beautifully decorated with dark-tinted markings. Some are evergreen, while those that are not retain their russet-tinted foliage throughout winter. Delicate spurred flowers emerge early in the year, and to allow these to be seen clearly the foliage should be sheared back in late winter.

Many exciting species of epimedium are being introduced from China, but so far none has proved hardy enough for conditions in cool-temperate areas, although some may prove successful in milder parts of Britain and North America. Meanwhile the hardier species mostly originating from around the Mediterranean Sea, together with their hybrids and cultivars, have provided many excellent plants for clothing the woodland floor.

My favourite for year-round effect is *Epimedium* x *perralchicum* 'Frohnleiten', which is a cross between *E. perralderianum* and *E. pinnatum* subsp. *colchicum*, both of which are also well worth growing in their own right. The relatively large leaves of *E.* x *perralchicum* 'Frohnleiten' have a bronze wash when this evergreen renews them in

ABOVE The foliage of *Epimedium* x *rubrum* (*below left*) looks attractive all summer, having developed immediately after its early spring flowering. In autumn and winter the leaves assume rich maroon tints (*below centre*). The evergreen foliage of *Epimedium* x *perralchicum* 'Frohnleiten' (*below right*) remains glossy green throughout the winter.

spring, but they quickly turn bright green with a characteristic shiny surface that gives them considerable impact in shady areas of the garden. In winter its foliage can again become tinted bronze, yet it always remains glossy and fresh. The bright yellow flowers are held well clear of the foliage in mid-spring.

Epimedium x *rubrum* is a pleasure to behold at every stage. It is more delicate than *E.* x *perralchicum* 'Frohnleiten' and has plain green, pointed leaves throughout summer. In winter these turn dark maroon and must be cut away early enough to allow their spring flowers to be fully appreciated. These are bright red with white spurs and dance in the air above the newly emerging foliage, which is pale green washed with pink. Quickly this strange leaf coloration darkens to a brick red that stands out in contrast to the fresh greens and yellows that tend to dominate the garden at this time of the year. *Epimedium* x *rubrum* is a hybrid between *E. alpinum* and the

Japanese species *E. grandiflorum*. A variety of this latter species, *E.g.* 'Lilafee', spreads quickly to form wide patches, which in spring are a mass of copper-coloured foliage below a cloud of lilac-purple flowers. When in flower this cultivar is quickly sold out in any nursery wise enough to stock it.

Epimedium grandiflorum has also been crossed with *E. pinnatum* subsp. *colchicum* to produce another group of excellent, fast-growing cultivars. *Epimedium* x *versicolor* 'Sulphureum' is offered by nearly every garden centre, and deservedly so. The green foliage is prettily decorated and marked, and the light yellow flowers are freely produced. In the case of *E.* x *v.* 'Versicolor', cherry-red buds open to soft pink flowers with light yellow centres, to create a copper-bronze effect from a distance.

One more epimedium not to be forgotten bears darker, copper-orange flowers and larger evergreen foliage. It is *E.* x *warleyense*

'Orangeköningin'. This hybrid between *E. pinnatum* subsp. *colchicum* and *E. alpinum* has a growth habit that is coarser and more open, and the plants quickly spread to make impressive carpets that remain effective well into winter – their leaves having developed a strong red hue as temperatures begin to fall.

The one thing that all epimediums have in common is their woodland character. By this I mean that they are delicate and airy. However they could never be used to create a formal, tidy, groundcover design. In contrast, another

splendid evergreen groundcover, *Tellima grandiflora* could be used more formally. Like epimediums, it develops rich foliage tints in winter but its rounded, scallop-shell-shaped, thickly textured leaves give it a solid regular appearance. They are layered over each other to form dense, ground-smothering clumps. Such plants are ideal for edging paths and filling spaces in both shade and sunlit areas of the garden. In spring slim flower stems bearing tiny green bells edged pale pink rise clear of their foliage. The effect is subtle rather than spectacular, and so fits perfectly

ABOVE *Tellima grandiflora* 'Purpurteppich' is sometimes grown primarily for its neat and attractive ground-hugging foliage rather than for its delicate flower spikes, which are produced in late spring.

within a woodland setting. Although *T. grandiflora* grows better in rich moist soils, it is also tolerant of dry shade and hence indispensable. It is far more reliable than the rather similar tiarellas and heucheras which are its close relatives. Of the various cultivars available, *T.g.* 'Rubra Group' is the classic form turning rich maroon in winter. *Tellima grandiflora* 'Purpurteppich' is a heavier stained form, which begins to show dark tones in its leaf venation during summer before turning sumptuous maroon in winter. Its flowers are also larger and more richly coloured, which is not necessarily an advantage. There is also a cultivar with flowers rich with a scent reminiscent of old-fashioned pinks. This is *T.g.* 'Oderata Group', which is less colourful in winter yet possibly the most sophisticated of them all to use in a wilder woodland garden.

For a change of texture, the straplike leaves of *Liriope muscari*, which are dark green and glossy, are ideal for edging paths in both shade and sunlit areas of the garden.

Spikes of violet-purple flowers rise some 30cm (1ft) above their arching foliage in late summer and can persist long into winter.

Woodrushes (*Luzula*) are far less exotic but equally useful, thriving in sun and shade. They become especially important when conditions are dry and difficult for most other ground-covering plants to establish and spread. *Luzula sylvatica* is the commonest. It has dark green, straplike leaves, edged with a fine yellow line in the form usually offered – *L.s.* 'Marginata'. My preference is for *L.s.* 'Tauernpass', with its broad, light green leaves arranged in ground-hugging rosettes.

Brunneras, pulmonarias, and pachyphragma are deciduous or, as in the case of the pulmonarias, become shabby and tattered in winter; as such they are not really the most effective groundcover for large areas. However, as part of a groundcover tapestry of plants they are invaluable for their foliage patterns and sparkling spring flowers. All are described in more detail within spring seasonal planting (*see pp.118–127*).

BELOW This tapestry of mixed groundcover plants is planted at a woodland edge. It includes leathery-leaved bergenias, several patches of epimediums, clumps of hellebores, and a drift of *Dicentra formosa* in the background.

Ferns

ABOVE The royal fern (*Osmunda regalis*) creates the dominant theme in this section of the Jac P. Thijsse Park, Amstelveen, The Netherlands.

While ferns are very much an essential part of the perennial garden, whether they can be developed into a conspicuous planting theme is less clear. They are associated with damp woodland and unless you can provide the conditions that ferns need to succeed they are unlikely to thrive. Scale is also a factor as only the largest and tallest-growing species are going to make an impact and be able to dominate the scene.

In the Jac P. Thijsse Park in Amstelveen, The Netherlands, it is royal fern (*Osmunda regalis*) that has relished the growing conditions of a high water table and acid soil to create stunning drifts under the shade of trees as well as in open, sun-drenched clearings. In spring the fronds emerge from bare soil in a display that can rival anything to be seen in a man-made sculpture exhibition. Daily they change and finally unfurl their dramatic wide fronds, which stand more than 1.5m (5ft) high. All summer long they are bold and green, but in late autumn the cold causes them to fade and develop russet tints before collapsing under a blanket of snow. In a small garden a single plant of royal fern might be interesting, but only when it is used on a truly large scale can its full potential be exploited.

Easier to accommodate in small garden spaces are the narrow, neat, erect shuttlecocks formed by *Matteuccia struthiopteris*, which stand 90cm (36in) high. This fern is also less pernickety about its growing conditions, although it does need plenty of moisture to reach its full potential. Using underground runners it spreads and quickly fills wide spaces. It is a good choice for a dramatic planting theme in a semi-shaded, woodland setting.

Tree ferns are the largest of all ferns, and even one plant can have a great impact on its surroundings. They come from cool rainforests in the southern hemisphere and are not truly hardy in cool-temperate climates. My own *Dicksonia fibrosa* had merged happily into a jumble of large perennials growing at the back of a border (*see p.45*), but in spring, surrounded by only tulips and lower-growing perennials, it looked so out of place that I was relieved when eventually it died following a particularly cold winter. Such exotic plants need the right setting, for example in a city-centre, courtyard garden, perhaps isolated from any natural vegetation and associated with other antipodean plants such as phormiums. However, in a larger country garden, tree ferns work best in a woodland setting that mimics their rainforest home.

Perhaps the best way to use the distinctive character of ferns in your garden is as accents within a mixed, woodland, groundcover planting. Rising out of drifts of epimediums or pulmonarias they can add height, contrast,

and interest, especially when different forms are repeated throughout the area.

No plant is worth growing unless it thrives, and many ferns require plenty of moisture and protection from wind to remain healthy and grow well. Although gardens are often too dry for these ferns, in many other respects the shade and shelter provided by nearby buildings and trees make the perfect setting for them. Fortunately, many ferns are far more drought tolerant than you might expect, and it is to this group that you should first look.

Top of my planting list will always be dryopteris. The toughest is the familiar male fern (*Dryopteris filix-mas*), because once established it is truly drought tolerant and perfect for the dry shady conditions associated with trees. Yet given moist soils it will readily grow 1m (3ft) tall and develop into an imposing specimen. Among the many selections to choose from are some with pinched and curled fronds, and these could be assembled into an interesting collection and effective planting theme.

Dryopteris affinis is very similar to male fern and is tolerant of sun and wind, making it one of the most easily placed in the garden. *Dryopteris affinis* 'Cristata', sometimes sold as *D.a.* 'Cristata The King', is one of the most elegant cultivars, with interestingly crested

ABOVE Despite its delicate appearance, *Polypodium vulgare* 'Cornubiense' is tough and evergreen.

BELOW The new fronds of *Dryopteris erythrosora* emerge a startling copper colour, which gradually fades to a fresh shade of shiny green for the remainder of the summer.

Geranium 'Brookside' and *Rosa* 'Ghislaine de Féligonde' receive enough light to flower in early summer, while ferns thrive in the shade cast by a newly planted copper beach hedge. The ferns are *Polystichum setiferum* Divisilobium Group 'Dahlem', with colourful *Dryopteris erythrosora* and upright *D. tokyoensis* just visible at the rear, in front of the geranium.

ends to the pinnae, which make up its long arching fronds, up to 90cm (36in) tall.

Dryopteris erythrosora is much lower growing than those already mentioned but is by no means less effective in a planting scheme. Its wide spreading fronds emerge in spring in the most intense shade of copper-orange. Eventually this fades to glossy green, but it never really loses its metallic sheen. As long as the soil is moist enough, this fern grows happily at the front of a sunny border, where it reaches 50cm (20in) tall.

A fern worth finding a place for is *D. wallichiana*, which matures into an impressive elegant clump. In spring it attracts a lot of attention when its fresh, golden-green foliage contrasts with its dark black, hairy stems. *Dryopteris tokyoensis* is another easily grown fern, with a very distinctive upright habit. The leaves are pale green and the stems black. Not only does it not need much space but it also makes an unusual accent plant because in ideal conditions it can grow more than 70cm (28in) tall.

Lady fern (*Athyrium filix-femina*) is almost as tough as male fern. Its common name refers to its delicate foliage, not to its constitution; nor is it in any way closely related to male fern. Lady fern's finely divided foliage is easily damaged by wind, and plants must have sufficient moisture to grow well. My own plant of *A. f.-f.* 'Grandiceps', with its infinitely divided, lacy foliage, struggled for years in a dry corner, but it never died. Now relocated, it thrives, and delights me with its freshness and delicacy all summer until the first frost, when it immediately departs the scene. There are numerous forms of lady fern to choose from, as well as other species of athyrium. I grow charming, dark-stemmed *A. vidalii* and Japanese painted fern (*A. niponicum* var. *pictum*). Japanese painted fern – one of the most popular ferns – has metallic-green foliage suffused with grey, blue, and pink, but at only 35cm (14in) tall it is more useful as an interesting accent than a central feature of a planting scheme.

Another group of ferns many gardeners could not do without are species of polystichum. These ferns are more drought tolerant than either dryopteris or athyrium, and mostly they are evergreen, which is a bonus. *Polystichum aculeatum* forms an attractive mound of glossy, dark green foliage, which is renewed around mid-spring each year. A little taller, to 60cm (2ft), is *P. polyblepharum*, which produces probably the shiniest leaves of any evergreen fern; again these are renewed each spring and

Tough, evergreen hart's tongue fern (*Asplenium scolopendrium*) has a bold simple shape, which looks good when used near the front of planting areas.

can readily be damaged by late frosts if not given a sheltered position.

Soft shield fern (*P. setiferum*) is not only one of the easiest garden ferns to grow but also one of the most attractive. Its typically dark green fronds are long and arching. A beautiful cultivar, *P.s.* 'Pulcherrimum Bevis', has its leathery leaves covered in silky filaments, while *P.s.* Foliosum Group produces rather more congested foliage. These two have the same growth habit, which makes them difficult plants to combine into any tightly packed, mixed border. They are best set apart, perhaps rising out of low-growing groundcover such as ajuga, *Galium oderatum*, or *Omphalodes cappadocica*. Alternatively, they can be used in a narrow bed between a house and a path, where their drought tolerance enables them to survive. In such a position they could freely display their arching foliage to perfection.

More upright in habit, and therefore more readily accommodated in a border, is *P. setiferum* Divisilobium Group 'Dahlem'. Being grown from spores not divisions, it is far less expensive and more widely available than many other soft shield ferns.

Polypodium is the real toughie of the fern world. *Polypodium vulgare* can grow as an epiphyte in mild areas, where it can be found thriving in the forks of trees. It will also grow

out of retaining walls, as will its even more drought-tolerant relatives *P. cambricum* and *P. interjectum*. The fronds of *P. interjectum* are longer and narrower than those of *P. vulgare* but have the same simple, deeply lobed structure. Tough and evergreen like the rest, the fronds of *P.v.* 'Cornubiense' (as it is called in garden centres) comprise numerous finely divided pinnae. It can also throw up normal fronds, which are best removed. All these polypodiums are best planted along path edges or among low-growing, groundcover plants.

Hart's tongue fern (*Asplenium scolopendrium*) is small but full of charm. It has the simplest leaf of all ferns – being long, thin, and undivided, although some selections have wavy edges to the fronds. In a corner, and of necessity right at the front, try *A.s.* 'Angustatum', which has very narrow fronds with slightly toothed edges.

As a group the ferns described here could easily be arranged into a planting theme that would be effective year round, because most are evergreen or nearly so. Their companions should be groundcover plants, such as epimediums, tellimas, woodrushes, liriopes, pulmonarias, brunneras, and hellebores, arranged into a tapestry of varying textures and flower colours. Bulbs could introduce an additional seasonal highlight in spring.

Waterside Perennials

Flowering hibiscus and ornamental grasses create a sense of enclosure for swimmers when they are using this circular swimming pool designed by James van Sweden.

Water on its own is a powerful design element in a garden, and you should be careful when planting around it to avoid running counter to the very functions for which it has been introduced. Paramount among these is its use to create an open space within the garden landscape. In this way it can counterbalance borders filled with plants as might also open areas of groundcover perennials, lawns, and even hard surfacing. The very nature of water controls the way you move around the spaces

in a garden, and this can be invaluable when you want to prevent progress in a particular direction yet avoid interrupting an interesting view.

These functional considerations aside, it is the reflective qualities of water and the possibility of introducing movement and sound within a garden that sets it apart. Fountains, waterfalls, and cascades add interest and excitement, and any planting associated with them should pick up the

marginal plants and water lilies gradually obliterate the mirror effect, which can bring reflections of clouds and sky down to ground level or might double the impact of any surrounding planting.

When there is space to spare in a garden, marginal aquatic plants are the obvious choice for creating a natural look; however, they encroach on the surface area of the pond and in a small garden this might be a waste of this special resource. Instead, planting outside the pond in the surrounding soil leaves open the maximum amount of water.

Waterside perennials fall into one of two groups: those that grow naturally in damp soils associated with water or marshes; and those plants that look as if they would grow in damp, waterside situations but which actually grow quite happily in drier soils. Whichever group of plants you choose, they should be arranged in bold sweeping masses that relate to the open plate of water they surround. You should therefore avoid mixing too many different-looking plants. This is a real danger when there are naturally damp conditions, because there are a host of glorious perennials that the collector in us would relish. Here you should be looking for plants that will create eye-catching effects in given seasons and situations.

Bold-leaved *Gunnera manicata* dominates this waterside planting, while red *Crocosmia* 'Lucifer' flourishes in the drier soil in the background.

mood. The grasses in the perennial meadow surrounding the old fountain at Scampston Hall (*see p.69*) seem to mimic its spreading form, for example. Next to a channel of fast-running water in an open situation *Pennisetum alopecuroides* might be a good choice. The wind might then whip it into a spectacle of ripples and streamers.

Still water is far more common in gardens and provides an opportunity to reflect the beauty that surrounds it. All too easily

RIGHT In dry soil in the foreground drought-tolerant, yellow *Coreopsis verticillata* and violet-blue perovskias grow happily. Nearer the water, ornamental grasses mimic the reeds and rushes to be found elsewhere, while eupatoriums and *Petasites japonicus* enjoy the damper soils at a lower level.

OPPOSITE *Astilbe chinensis* var. *davidii* has been planted in the foreground with *A.* 'Rotlicht' behind in this design. These are just two of many hundreds of astilbes that can be combined in a woodland setting to create a sensational summer planting theme.

Bold displays of candelabra primulas bring the Fairhaven gardens in Norfolk, England alive during late spring (*see pp.55 and 125*). Earlier the extraordinary yellow flowers of *Lysichiton americanus* and its Chinese equivalent in white, *L. camtschatcensis*, will have emerged from the mud along the sides of the same meandering watercourses. By late spring these will have formed huge paddle leaves to fill the background.

Strong foliage shapes are perhaps the most dramatic style of planting used to contrast with the ubiquitous stands of vertical reeds and rushes that are often to be found in such situations. The size of dramatic gunneras makes them suitable for only the largest gardens. For smaller ones you should consider other large-leaved perennials such as *Darmera peltata*, with its rounded leaves following its earlier flower display. Rodgersias produce fingerlike leaves and flowers in mid-summer, and ligularias have scalloped leaves sometimes in dark hues that can bring an element of surprise in late summer, when their dramatic spikes of yellow, starlike flowers appear. As a group, these plants create the lush background that gardeners associate with such damp places, and their flowers bring with them a seasonal bonus.

Astilbes are grown primarily for their flower display. Where conditions allow, these are undoubtedly the best choice to create dramatic colour drifts. In my own garden I am limited to using *Astilbe chinensis* var. *taquetii*

'Purpurlanze', which is tolerant of drier than average garden soil, but it would be with the range of rich-hued arendsii hybrids that I would work given the opportunity. A tapestry in shades of pinks and purples would make up the mid-summer spectacle. After flowering these plants develop attractive, plume-shaped seed heads that look good for many months.

The soil beside a pool, pond, or artificial water feature may be fairly dry if it is separated from the water by a waterproof lining. Although succulents and cacti growing next to such artificial water basins do not look out of place, undoubtedly the most appropriate planting choices are species that look at least as if they should relish damp waterside margins. Fortunately, some of the large-leaved perennials, including darmera, rodgersia, hosta, and ligularia, can be grown successfully in well-drained soil as long as it is moist throughout the year. However, summer irrigation might be needed.

A more successful planting scheme next to an artificial water basin will be plants truly adapted to such drier conditions but which look, in habit, similar to those plants that naturally grow in and around water. Ornamental grasses are a good choice, as are strap-leaved phormiums that mimic reeds and rushes. Likewise, *Helianthus salicifolius* which, as its name suggests, has fine foliage like a waterside willow, looks graceful in such a position, especially when its shape is reflected in still water.

Ornamental Grasses

Grasses with their long, thin, flexible foliage have a very recognizable character all of their own, so much so that other plants with a similar growth habit are sometimes referred to as grasslike. The linear leaf patterns on grasses contrast attractively with neighbouring, broad-leaved plants. Any associations you make with the open countryside, prairie, or savannah will all add to the effective use of grasses in the garden.

I first became aware of ornamental grasses some 20 years ago in photographs of North American gardens and public spaces in which grasses were planted in an extensive way. These wide drifts of grasses made a reference to the tall grass prairies which at one time had dominated the North American landscape. Not only was the scale of these plantings new to me but also the plants

LEFT A gossamery veil is created by *Molinia caerulea* subsp. *arundinacea* 'Transparent' when it throws up its long flower stems in mid-summer. If it is planted with *Monarda* 'Pawnee', as here, the combination provides not only early season colour but also late season, seed-head contrasts.

RIGHT It is the textures and contrasts that ornamental grasses bring to perennial planting schemes which make them so important. Here the golden cloud is created following the flowering of *Deschampsia cespitosa* 'Goldtau' in early summer. The arching green mound of silky foliage made by *Hakonechloa macra* is effective from the moment it comes into leaf through into winter, when it is flushed first by light lemon tints and eventually by soft tans.

A recent addition to the grass assortment is *Pennisetum orientale* 'Tall Tails', which can reach more than 1.5m (5ft) tall. The flowers are flushed pink when they appear in summer and eventually turn white. They are seen here growing alongside *Astilbe chinensis* var. *taquetii* 'Purpurlanze'.

themselves were unfamiliar to most British gardeners at that time.

Things were destined to change, and one man in particular can be held responsible. Ernst Pagels has become a legend in his own lifetime through the way he has discovered perennial plants that are now considered indispensable by gardeners. *Salvia nemorosa* 'Ostfriesland', *Achillea* 'Credo', *Rodgersia podophylla* 'Rotlaub', *Eupatorium purpureum* subsp. *maculatum* 'Riesenschirm', *Inula magnifica* 'Sonnenstrahl', and *Stachys officinalis* 'Hummelo' are just some of the perennials with which he is connected, and then of course there are his grasses. Ernst Pagels realized that *Miscanthus sinensis* had great potential as a landscaping plant but that in cool-temperate areas it hardly ever flowered. In regions with longer and hotter summers such as North America, this species flourished, and so he set about developing

cultivars that could cope with the cool wet climate of his native northern Germany. After more than 20 years work he had created a range of plants that could thrive in the cool-temperate climate of western Europe. He also discovered considerable variation of form and habit in the genetic makeup of a single species.

Other nurserymen have since contributed to the current wide range of grasses suitable for a host of situations and uses. There are bushy forms such as *M.s.* 'Kleine Fontäne', to 1.6m (5¼ft) tall, which is ideal for planting in blocks or as hedges and is one of the best ornamental grasses for a small garden. Some of the tallest, such as *M.s.* 'Silberturm', *M.s.* 'Nishidake', and *M.s.* 'Sirene', grow to more than 3m (10ft) tall and are invaluable background plants or specimens in the open landscape. The fine, white-variegated leaves of *M.s.* 'Morning Light' are squeezed into narrow columns no more than 1.7m (5½ft)

RIGHT Because it is effective for at least ten months of the year, *Calamagrostis* x *acutiflora* 'Karl Foerster' has to be one of the most useful ornamental grasses in any planting scheme.

BELOW In exposed locations, grasses are an excellent choice, as here, where *Miscanthus sinensis* 'Kleine Fontäne' can sway freely in the wind.

BELOW RIGHT Stiffly upright *Miscanthus sinensis* 'Ghana' develops rich foliage tints as cooler autumn approaches.

tall to make focal points within a planting scheme, while in contrast the fine, rich green leaves of *M.s.* 'Krater' arch out extravagantly to cover many square metres of ground.

I have used many different cultivars of miscanthus to create a design that is dominated by their flower heads in late summer, but is interwoven with a range of late flowering perennials for contrast and relief. By early autumn, the plants unite into a single floral display, but what fascinates me is how different they are from one another. The broad green leaves of *M.s.* 'Zwergelefant' hang limply alongside the stiff, upright, bamboolike pillars of *M.s.* 'Sarabande'. The spidery flower heads of *M.s.* 'Undine' are held stiffly upright, while those of *M.s.* 'Kaskade' and *M.s.* 'Flamingo' arch over gracefully. Some, such as *M.s.* 'Pünktchen', even have golden-banded foliage and unlike the older cultivars, *M.s.* 'Strictus' and *M.s.* 'Zebrinus',

it also flowers profusely. Some flowers are the colour of red mahogany and pink icing sugar, while others are white or cream. Although individually they differ, when in flower they unite into a spectacular planting theme. Tossed by the wind and caught by the light, they bring drama and excitement to the field of yellow blooms, including rudbeckias and heleniums, that surrounds them. Later, in autumn, they create the setting for an extravagant display of colourful asters, and they continue to decorate the garden with their stiff silhouettes throughout winter.

Miscanthus are members of a group termed warm-season grasses, as they need warmth to start growing. In cool-temperate areas they tend to be slow to make a start in spring, they flower in late summer, and continue to be effective on into autumn. The same plants in warmer climates come into flower earlier. Other important

ABOVE *Stipa calamagrostis* is at home in a sunny, well-drained position, such as in this raised bed with fleshy sedums, silver-leaved artemisias, and violet-blue salvias. It is sometimes called *Achnatherum calamagrostis*.

warm-season grasses include pampas grass (*Cortaderia*), purple moor grass (*Molinia*), switch or Indian grass (*Panicum*), and fountain grass (*Pennisetum*). These are all indispensable for designing bold planting schemes with a late season of interest.

Panicum virgatum in particular is increasingly popular with gardeners. The various cultivars of this imposing upright grass reach 0.9–1.5m (36–60in) tall when in flower. *Panicum virgatum* 'Shenandoah' is the best of the forms noted for the red tints that develop in their mature foliage. Other selections produce blue-grey foliage. Of these *P.v.* 'Prairie Sky' is currently the best, but nurseries continue to seek even bluer and more impressive forms. Panicums are native to North America and together with other tall-growing grasses associated with the prairies, such as andropogon, schizachyrium, and sorghastrum, seem an appropriate choice for naturalistic planting schemes there.

Conversely, cold-season grasses become dormant when temperatures rise too high, and they begin growing and flower when cooler conditions prevail. Important examples of these are *Calamagrostis* x *acutiflora*, deschampsia, festuca, *Hakonechloa macra*, *Milium effusum*, and stipa. Such grasses play an important role in many spring and summer planting schemes, because they provide that important element of contrast to their broad-leaved companions. Stipas in particular are increasingly popular, with *S. gigantea* becoming almost a cliché in British gardens. Its tall golden flower heads seem to float like clouds above planting schemes as different as formal rose gardens and contemporary naturalistic perennial beds and borders.

Sedges and woodrushes tend to be grouped with true ornamental grasses as they are similar in character and are used in the same way in the garden. Sedges are species and cultivars of carex, and in evolutionary terms they are older than grasses. Most sedges grow as arching clumps of evergreen foliage in damp and shady situations.

Exceptions to this are the brown-leaved sedges from New Zealand, which need sunny open situations. Woodrushes are members of the genus *Luzula*. These low-growing, evergreen rushes are extremely tough. They can tolerate drought and shade, making them excellent as groundcover in difficult situations such as under tree canopies and next to buildings that cast rain shadows.

Other grasslike plants may include the popular, evergreen, groundcover *Liriope muscari*, black-leaved *Ophiopogon planiscapus* 'Nigrescens', irises (especially *Iris sibirica*), and possibly daylilies (*Hemerocallis*). Even though these may flower, it is their leaf patterns that distinguish them and impart a long effective season in any planting scheme.

TOP Blue *Festuca glauca* and red *Imperata cylindrica* 'Rubra' grasses make an exciting contrast with a fleshy-leaved sedum.

ABOVE As winter approaches the curved leaves of *Miscanthus sinensis* 'Gracillimus' turn shades of buff and tan and then stand as silhouettes for as long as weather conditions allow.

Index

Page numbers in italics refer to picture captions

Author's Acknowledgments

I would like to thank the garden owners, organisations and designers listed below for their assistance in making this book; without the images of their gardens my story would have been impossible to tell.

The team at Mitchell Beazley have worked tirelessly to ensure the accuracy and quality of my text and photographs. In particular the support from Michèle Byam, my commissioning editor and Victoria Burley on the graphic design side is greatly appreciated.

Ton Weesepoel, has once more supported this project throughout; aiding me on numerous photographic forays and in assisting with the final selection of images for this book.

The hospitality and free exchange of information from all those who have assisted me has made working on *The Perennial Garden* a pleasure – thank you all.

All photographs are by Michael King, who would like to thank the following:

d designer, t top, c centre, b bottom, l left, r right

4–5, 36c, 40, 80, 89b Stockholm, Sweden d Ulf Nordfjell; 2–3, 8-9, 32, 69, 71t, 86-7, 92, 93b, 133t, 136l, 137b, 141, 184, 185 Scampston Hall, North Yorkshire, UK, Sir Charles & Lady Legard, d Piet Oudolf; 6–7 Munich, Germany d Heiner Luz; 10–11, 168 Van Sweden residence, Maryland, USA d Oehme & Van Sweden Associates; 12–13, 16–17, 56, 78–9, 187t Millenium Park, Chicago, USA d Piet Oudolf; 14 Jacobs residence, Washington DC, USA d Oehme & Van Sweden Associates; 15, 65t, 66t, 167, 180 Sorg residence, Maryland, USA d Oehme & Van Sweden Associates; 18, 182bl Chicago Botanic Garden, USA d Oehme & Van Sweden Associates; 19, 24b, 45, 85b, 89t, 118, 120, 121b, 122, 123t, 124tl, 128, 131, 142, 146, 154–63, 178; Zonnehoek, Amsterdam, The Netherlands, Ton Weesepoel d Michael King; 20–1, 28t, 38-39, 52t, 70, 82–3, 139, 152tr, 171t Bury Court, Hampshire, UK, John Coke d Piet Oudolf; 22, 23, 108; Bury Court, Hampshire, UK, John Coke d Christopher Bradley-Hole; 24–5, 100–01 Waltham Place, Berkshire, UK, Mr & Mrs N F Openheimer d Henk Gerritsen; 26, 52br, 74–5, 95b 104–05, 106–07, 123b, 129, 134, 136r, 137t Hermannshof, Weinheim, Germany d Cassian Schmidt; 27, 66b Buga 2005, Munich, Germany; 28c and b, 68, 132, 164–5 Glen Chantry, Essex, UK, Mr. & Mrs. W. G. Staines; 30, 72–3, 168–69 Brillembourg residence, Maryland, USA d Oehme & Van Sweden Associates 31 Van Elburg, Sassenheim, NL d Piet Oudolf, the Netherlands; 33t, 63 Bramdean House, Hampshire, UK, Mr and Mrs H Wakefield; 34-35, 36t, 51, 59b, 84, 166, 173, Broughton Grange, Oxfordshire, UK d Tom Stuart-Smith; 37, 99b private estate, Hampshire, UK; 41–3 Riem Park, Munich, Germany d Heiner Luz; 44 Kasteeltuinen Arcen, The Netherlands; 46,

71b Brockhampton Cottage, Herefordshire, UK, Mr & Mrs Peter Clay d Tom Stuart-Smith; 47, 59t, 76, 96, 181 Lady Farm, Somerset, UK, Malcolm and Judy Pearce d Judy Pearce & Mary Payne; 48–9 Pelz residence, Magdeburg, Germany d Petra Pelz; 50, 98, 99c, 176 Jac. P. Thijsse Park, Amstelveen, The Netherlands; 52bl, 53, 110 Beth Chatto Gardens, Essex, UK; 54, 60b, 119t Great Dixter, East Sussex, UK, Christopher Lloyd; 55, 124tr, 125 Fairhaven Woodland & Water Garden, Norfolk, UK; 57t Amsterdam, The Netherlands d Jacqueline van der Kloet; 57b National Theatre, London, UK; 58t, Sleightholmedale Lodge, North Yorkshire, UK, Dr. & Mrs. O. James; 61, 170 Schloss Dyck, Jüchen, Germany; 62 Colemore House, Hampshire, UK, Mr and Mrs Simon de Zoete; 64 Informatietuinen Appeltern, The Netherlands; 65b Informatietuinen Appeltern, The Netherlands d Michael King; 67 Arlanda airport, Stockholm, Sweden d Ulf Nordfjell; 77t Weihenstephan Staudensichtungsgarten, Freising, Germany; 81, 112, 150, 151b, 186 Anja and Piet Oudolf residence, the Netherlands; 85t Tom Stuart-Smith residence, Hertfordshire, UK; 88 Cothay Manor, Somerset, UK, Mr. & Mrs. Alastair Robb; 90t, 138, Merriments Gardens, East Sussex, UK; 90b Stockholm, Sweden d Bernadette Schillings; 91t, 179 Hadspen House, Sommerset, UK, Sandra & Nori Pope; 91b Simon & Antonia Johnson residence, Somerset, UK; 93t Mein Ruys Tuinen, Dedemsvaart, the Netherlands d. Mein Ruys; 94, 171b Kasteeltuinen Arcen, the Netherlands; 95t private residence, San Francisco, California, USA d Ron Herman; 97t Hudson River Park, New York, USA d Oehme & Van Sweden Associates; 97b Chicago Botanic Garden, USA – Spider Island d Michael Van Valkenburgh; 102–03, 183 Fort Hooftddijk, University of Utrecht, the Netherlands; 111t Wisley Gardens, Royal Horticultural Society, UK d. Piet Oudolf; 113t Blackthorn Nurseries, UK, Mr and Mrs Robin White; 115 Braak, the Netherlands; 133b Simon Vogelaar, Steenderen, the Netherlands; 188 Potsdam, Germany d. Christian Meyer and Christine Orel.